NEW MEXICO

Volume 2
by
Ed Samuels

Samuels Studios
Product Design by Jim Samuels

Samuels, Ed
New Mexico Volume 2

ISBN-13: 978-1505459975
ISBN-10: 1505459974
$12.95
CreateSpace
U.S.A.

Printed in United States of America

The Cover

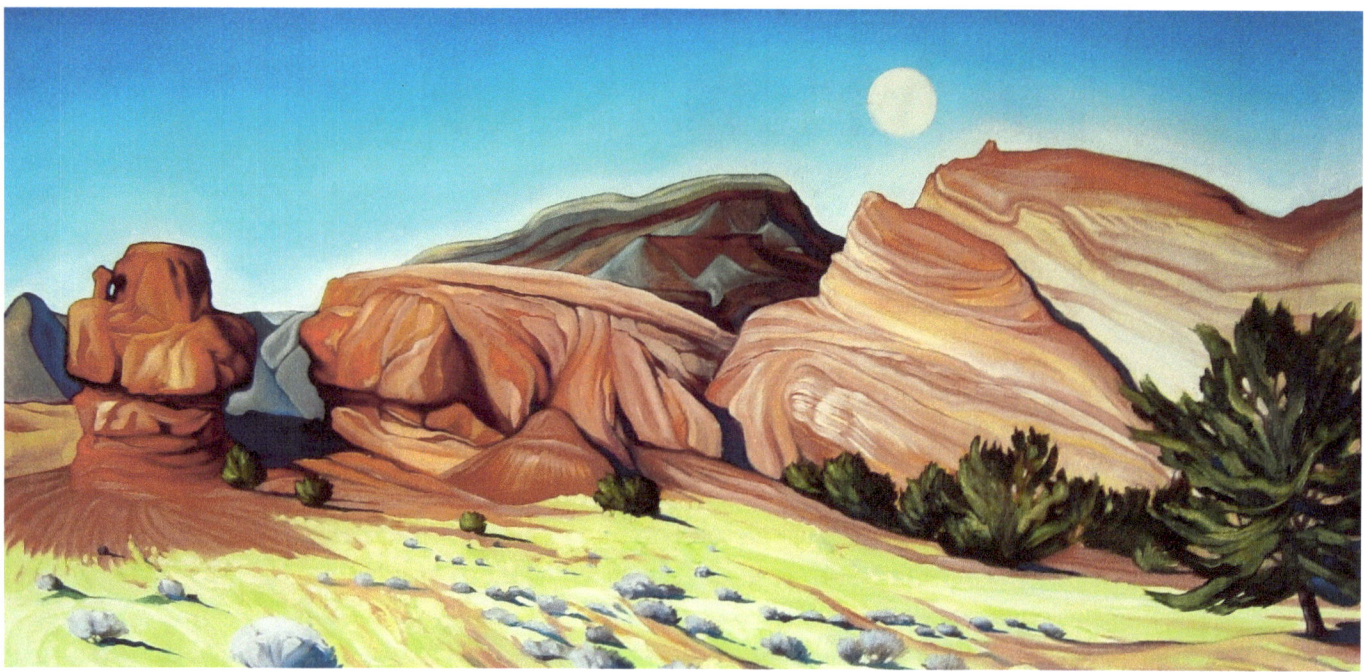

This is the first painting I did in the Jemez Mountains 32 years ago. I did it as the sun was going down and the moon was rising. I was driving my 1965 Mustang convertible. I set up my portable easel on the trunk of my car and went for it. Little did I know that there was no image making allowed on Pueblo lands. Later, when I took the time to read the signs, I got it. However, no one said a thing to me. In fact, several Indians had stopped to talk, and tell me good things about my efforts. Later, when a friend went out to paint them, he was told to pack up and leave. For myself, I just had a good time, and afterwards just counted my blessings.

Dear Reader,
I want to share with you a note I received from one of my dear patrons, as well as my response. I hope it reveals what it is that urges me to live the life of an artist, and how important sharing my art is to me and the people who come to own it.

- His note regarding the piece he acquired -

"Dear Ed, A most essential element to my well-being for these past 25 years. Inseparable, from the moment we met. Any story you'd find time to share would be great to experience."

- My Response -

"I was driving over the Via Grande one afternoon in 1988 I believe, when I experienced this amazing vision of these fall colors and composition of shapes. I stopped the car and did a quick sketch, then raced back to the studio where I did a small oil sketch immediately, and then the next morning a much larger painting.

"It was one of those out of body moments when the vision is all. Moments in the bath of creative energy every artist lives for. And, in the course of execution, wishes to share with others. Just how many of these moments we as artists have contributes to the whole of the person, and to the success of the drive and visual internal health that helps the source to create.

"Just how many paintings I have done, and how many have homes elsewhere in the world, I have no real idea. Hearing from someone that is living with one of my works, makes it even more worthwhile to me. It brings home to me just how successful my endeavors are, Recently, I uncovered a 24"X30" version of that work, and have it hanging on my stairwell wall. Thank you for the note. Great to share. ~Ed"

"Happy trails to you..."

Early spring blossoms in contrast to a old adobe which had recently been torn down. As well as a giant cottonwood tree. Often times I record these old adobe homes which disappear with all their charm and native spirit. Only to be replaced with doublewide prefab homes. They are so personalized, so different, each and every one. They express the character of those that built them in another era. One of independence and self reliance, built from the earth around them. The play of light and condition of the weather's effect on them, give me the artistic inspiration to try to capture the mood and personality of this lovely New Mexican way of life, Which is fast disappearing, melting back into the earth turning into history before my artists eye.

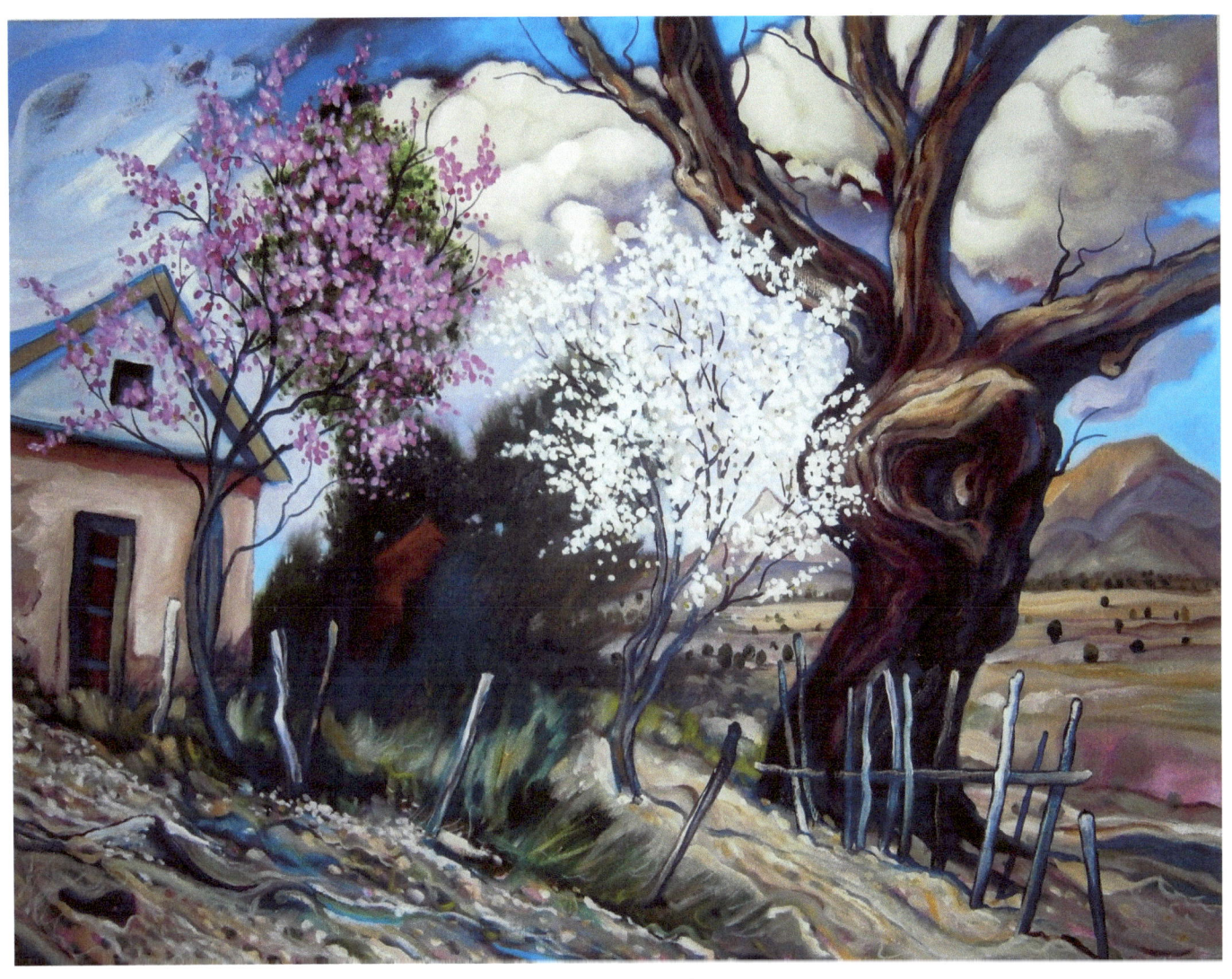

Old & New

Oil on canvas 30x40
2014

One of my favorite views showing the desert landscape in contrast to the waterways of New Mexico. Just before sunset this roadside attraction is always inspirational to me. The play of the light and the dark shadows animate the landscape with a clarity that always make me take brush in hand to try and capture the moment.

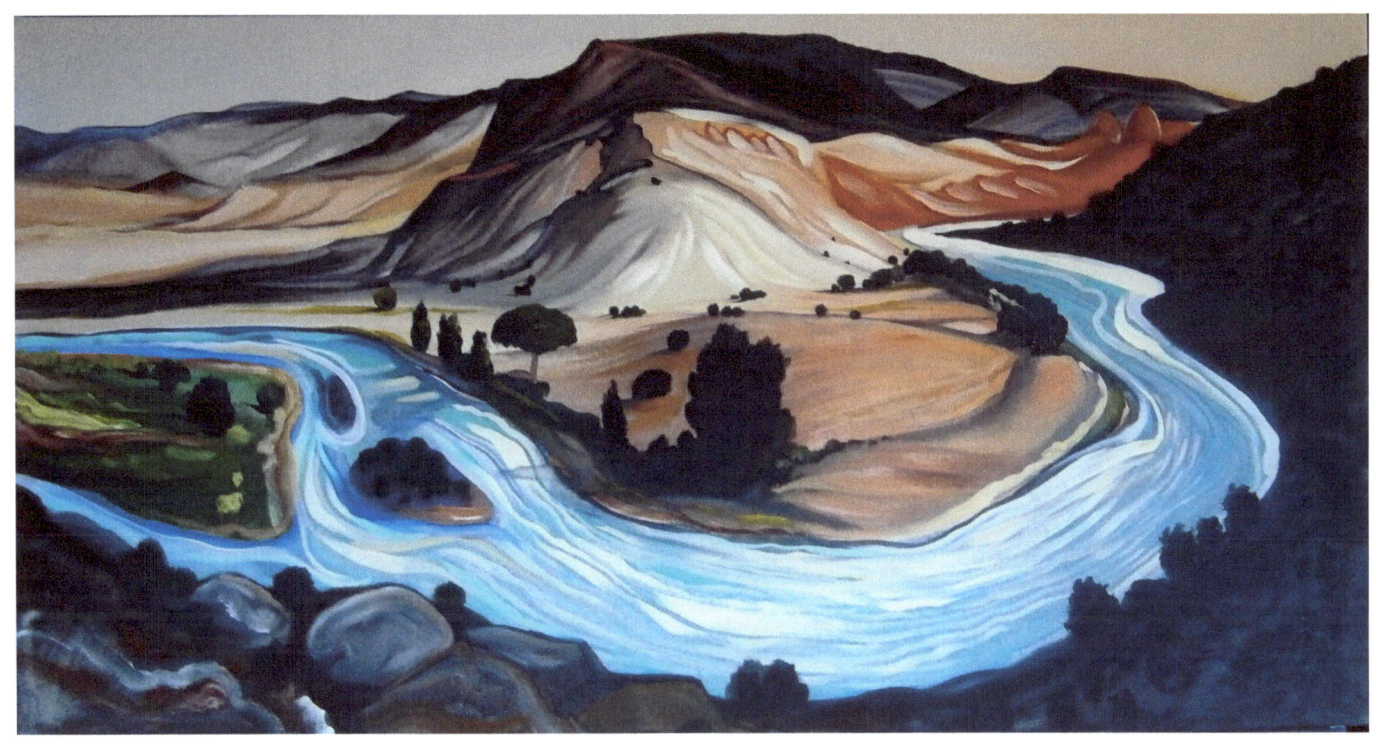

Rio Chama

Oil on canvas 26 X 60
2014

I see these two every time I approach the bridge over the Jemez River. They have been in my life 30 years now. Every year and every season they change. And I never cease to be amazed at their stoic beauty. They were big when I first moved here, and have had limbs break and fall; been covered in snow, and a pink green of new growth. But here they are turning golden with the cooler weather. A feast of change, and always catching the imagination. The changes they have silently witnessed, I can only wonder about.

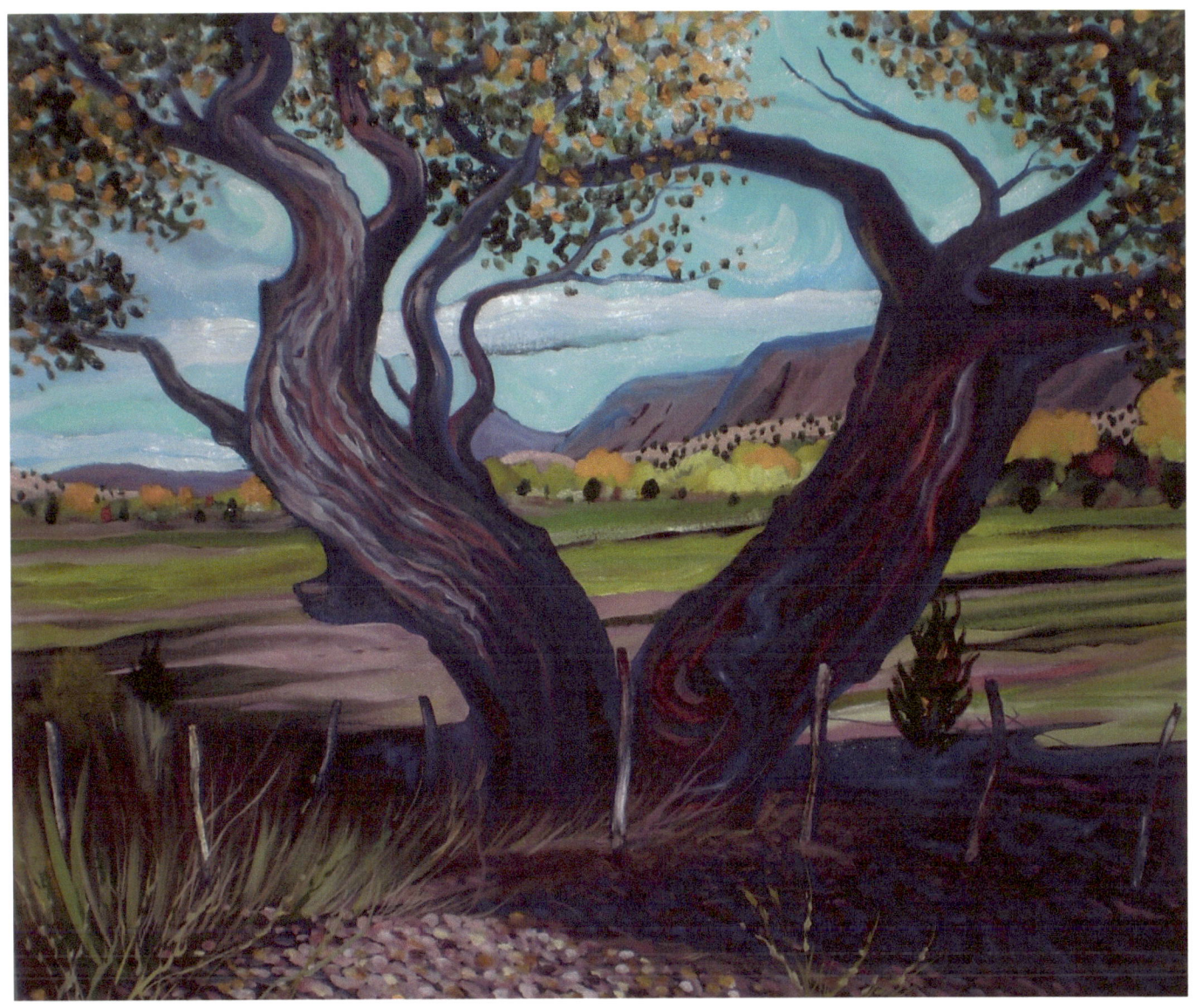

Old Twins

Oil on canvas 24 x 30
2014

A very lovely late summer feast of colors rampant on their front yard with the river behind. So, what was not to paint?

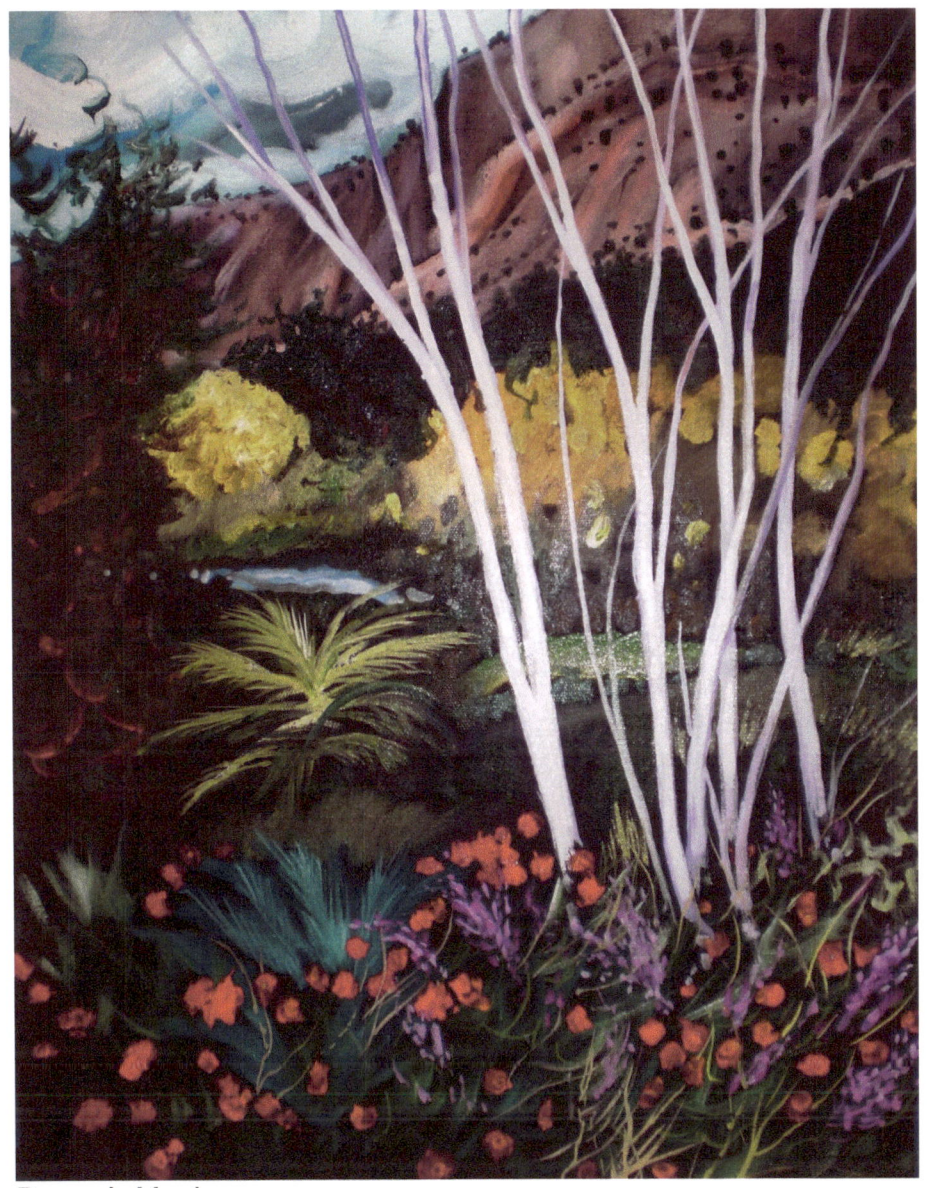

Dagna's Yard

Oil on canvas 16x20
2014

Every time one drives into Santa Fe, over the last hills from the south on the old Camino Real Road to the west, one sees the hill La Tatilla. The dance of light is always amazing. I have stopped my car several times, and if I have my paints, just paint it. Other times, I will take a photo and when home in the studio, paint it. At about two miles away it makes a perfect model, and I have painted it a lot.

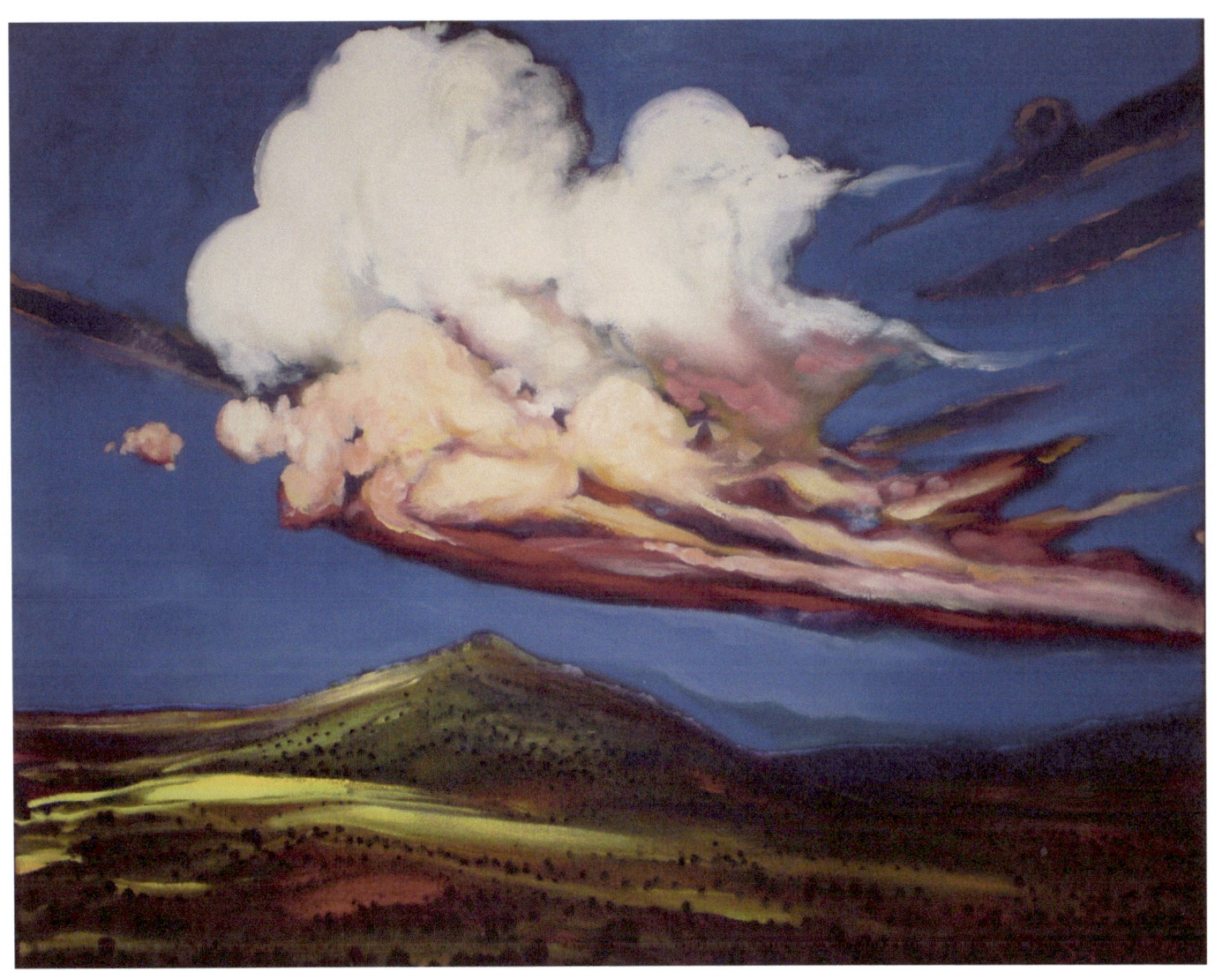

Thunder Head / La Tatilla

Oil on canvas 22x24
2014

This is the road to my home, under water. It was during one of those crazy wild pre-spring storms where the sky just opens up and dumps on the high mountain desert. I love them for their energy, although I have had floods in my home from them. After 30 years here, I still paint them all the time. I tried here to paint the landscape with the same energy the storm had, and from my memory of it.

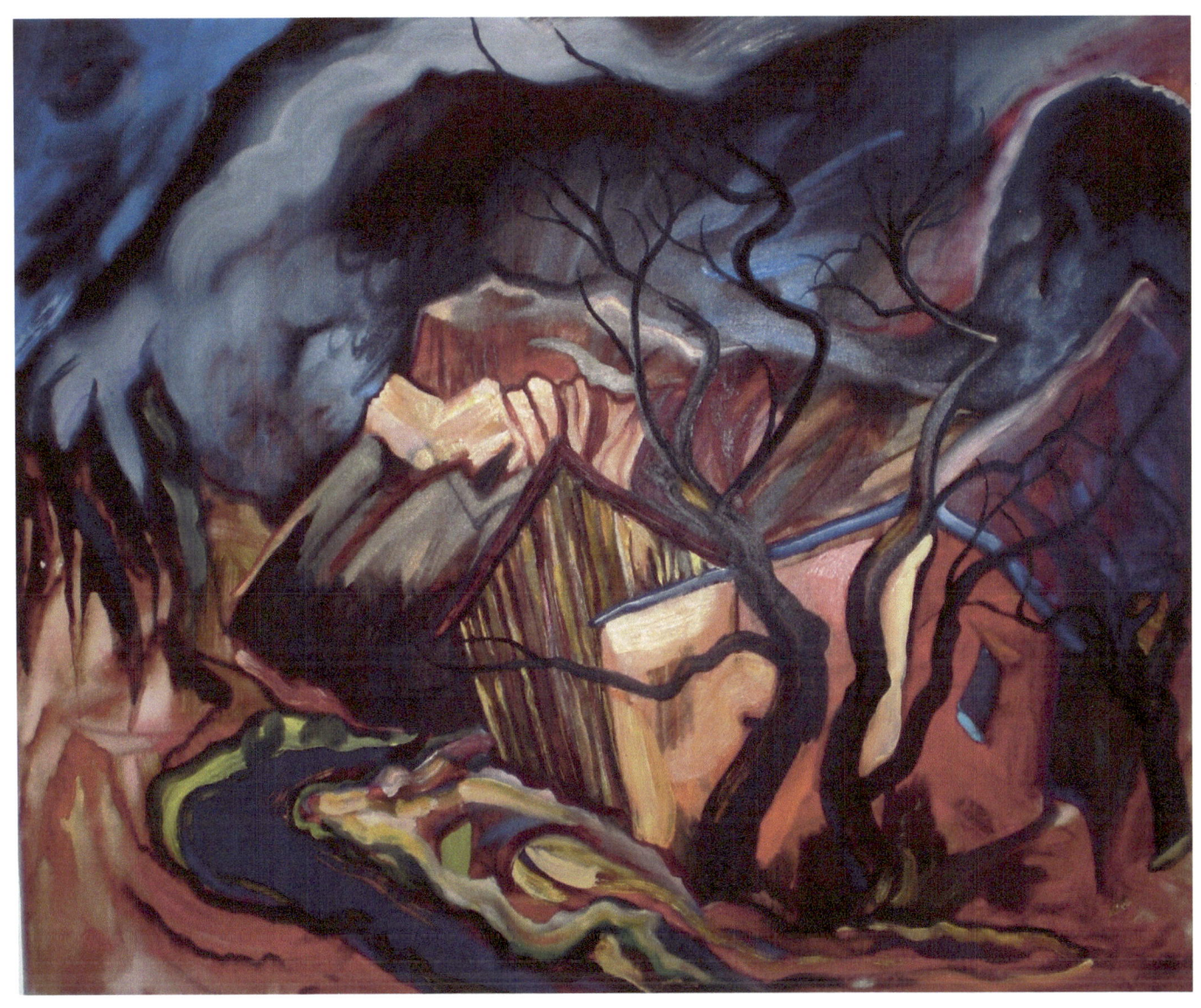

Crazy Storm

Oil on canvas 24x30
2014

An abstracted view of one of my favorite subjects. I just let it go and mixed the palette up and abstracted the interaction of the planes, intersecting them with color and perspective at my whimsical moods desire. More of an artistic intellectual approach. Having fun playing with my painter's roots in abstraction.

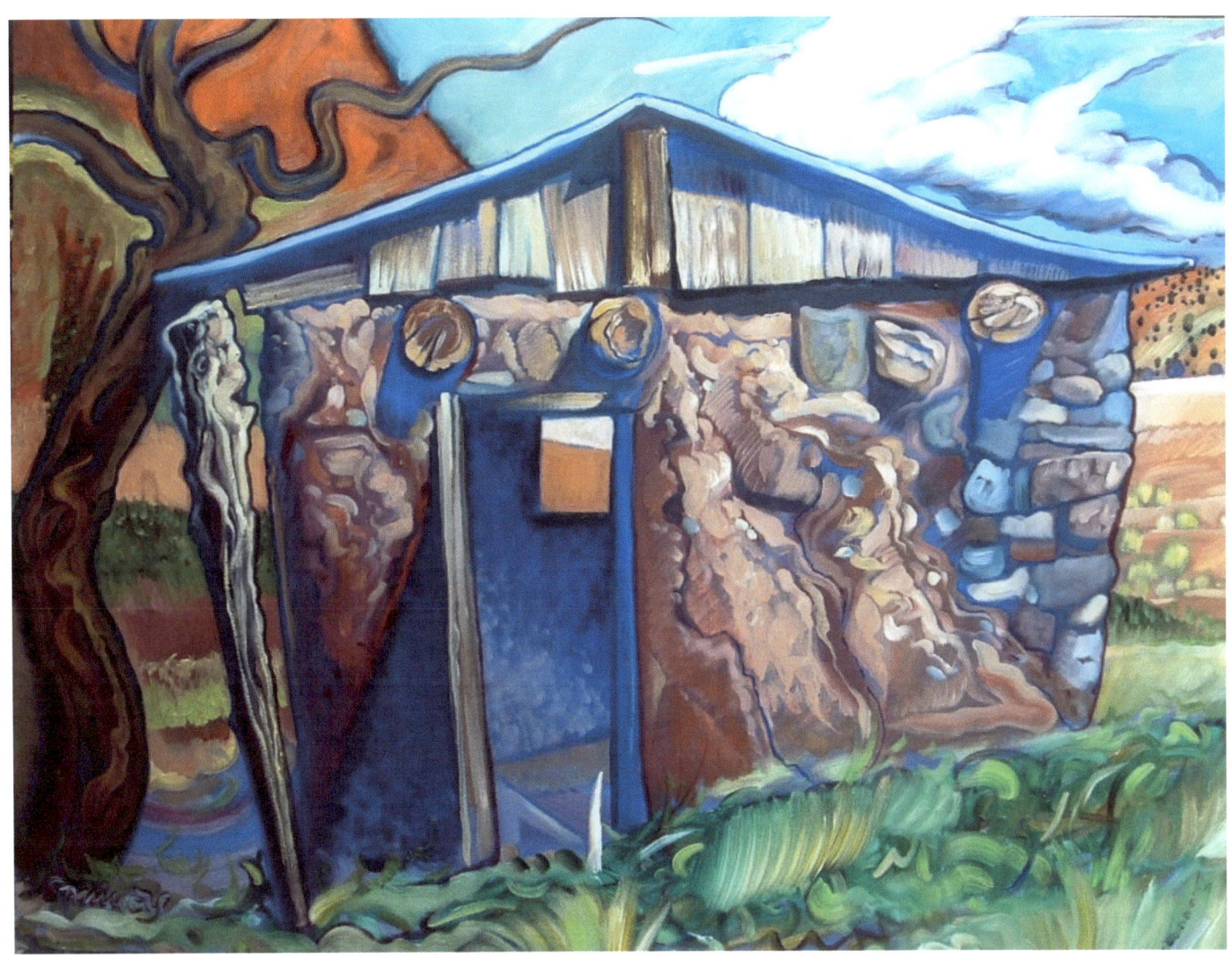

Anita's shed window

Oil on canvas 40x50
2014

A rear view of the river in Santa Fe. Normally it is dry. However, this year they let it run for a while. It was so beautiful with the lacework of foliage, and the sunlight's reflections making the river flow like a living being in a almost jungle-like canopy. I could hardly wait to get my easel and paint from my studio and paint it.

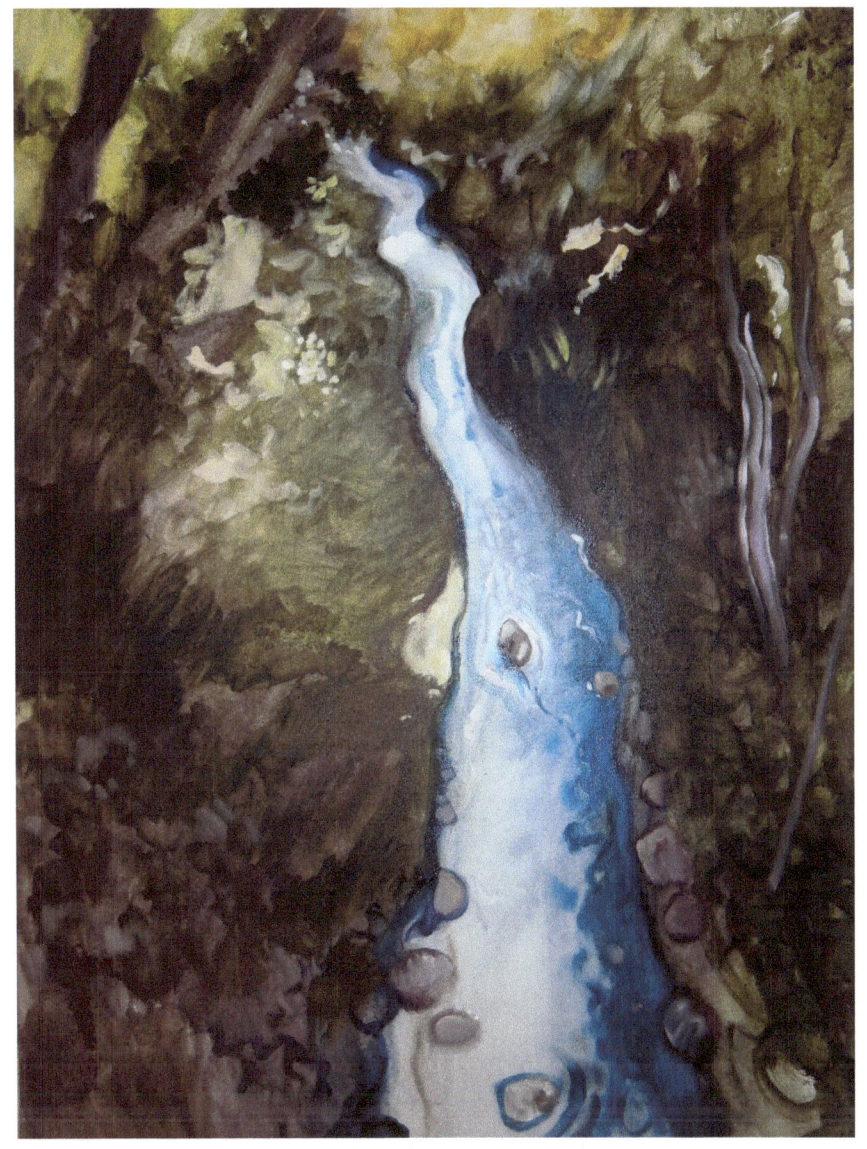

Bridge View

Oil on canvas 40x30
2014

The light was so intense on the Jemez River this one day when I stopped to take a walk on the bank of the river. It took me aback to see the crazy perspective making the river look as if it was running backwards. I worked on this painting doing my best to capture the feeling of the visual confusion I felt. I think I happily captured the feeling I got.

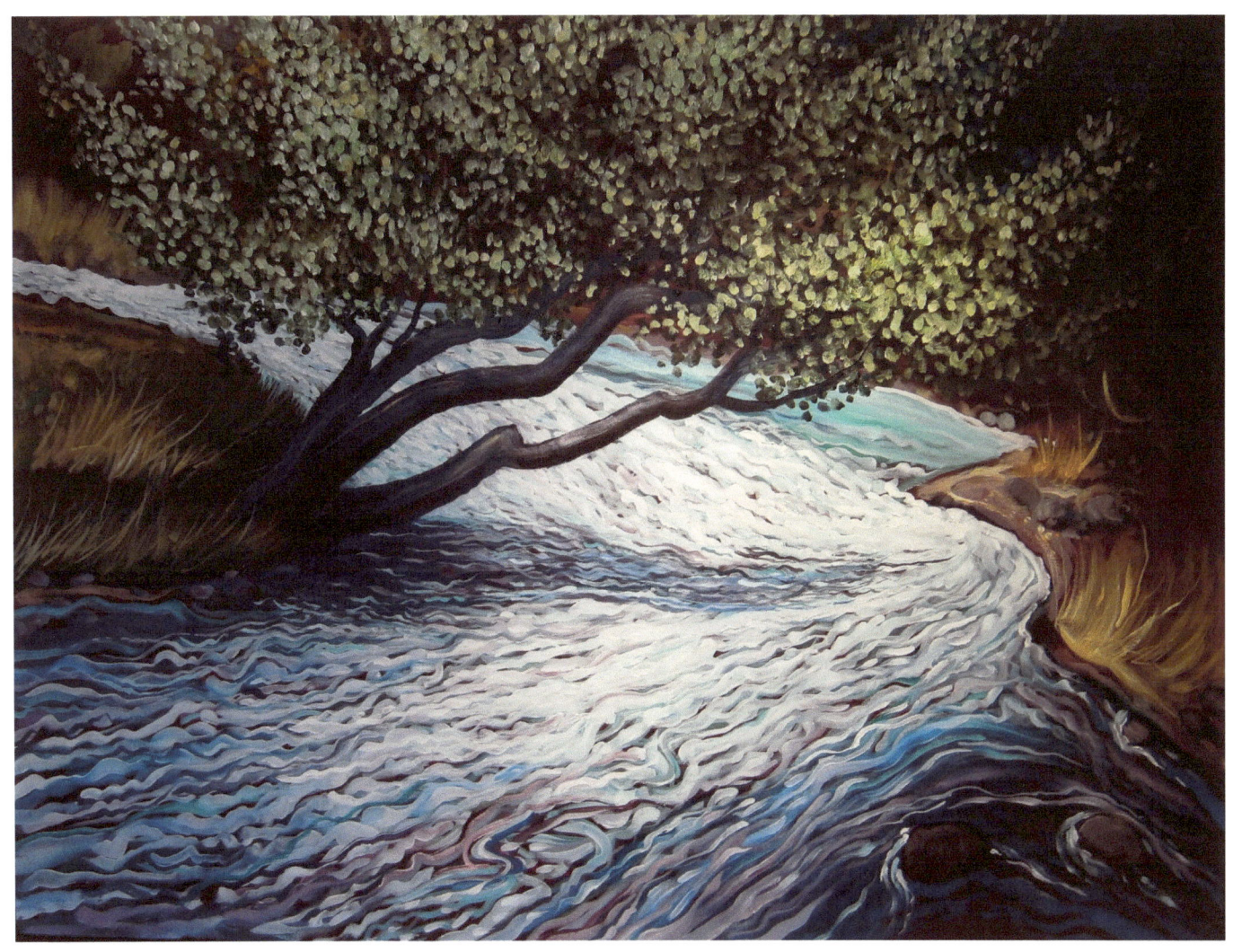

River's Bend

Oil on canvas 30x40
2014

One of the many abandoned adobes on my little traveled road, which always gave me the feeling it was getting ready to slide down the hill into the river. Very plastic in the approach, trying to give it the feeling of moving, of the weight of the earth and time.

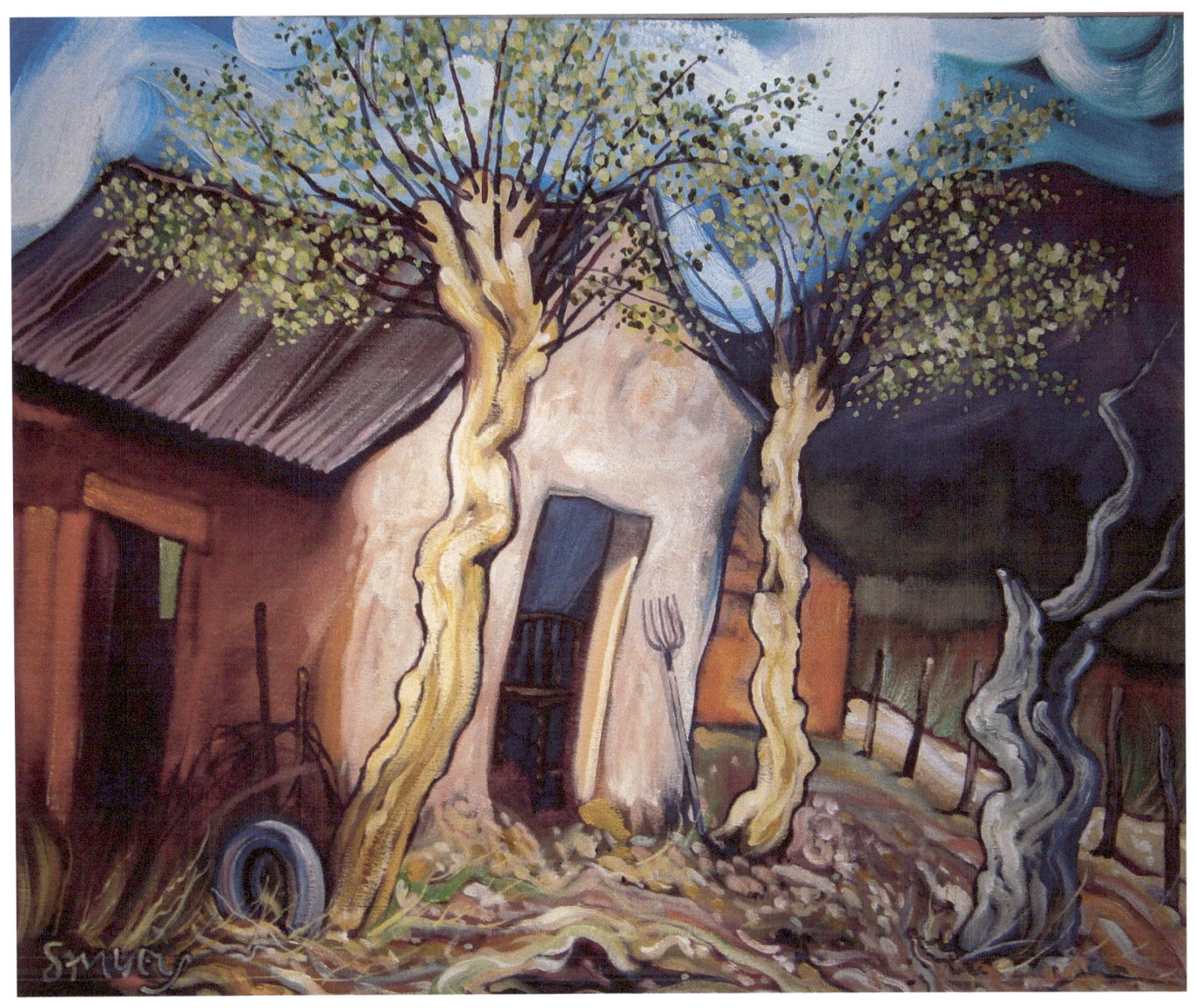

Forgotten Now

Oil on canvas 24x30
2014

It was so hot that summer, and the Jemez Mountains were on fire for a month. Seventy-six miles long, oppressively obvious to all. I consoled myself by painting the forest in a state of heavy spring runoff, to just feel cooler and take my mind off the horror of the earth burning in such an explosive matter.

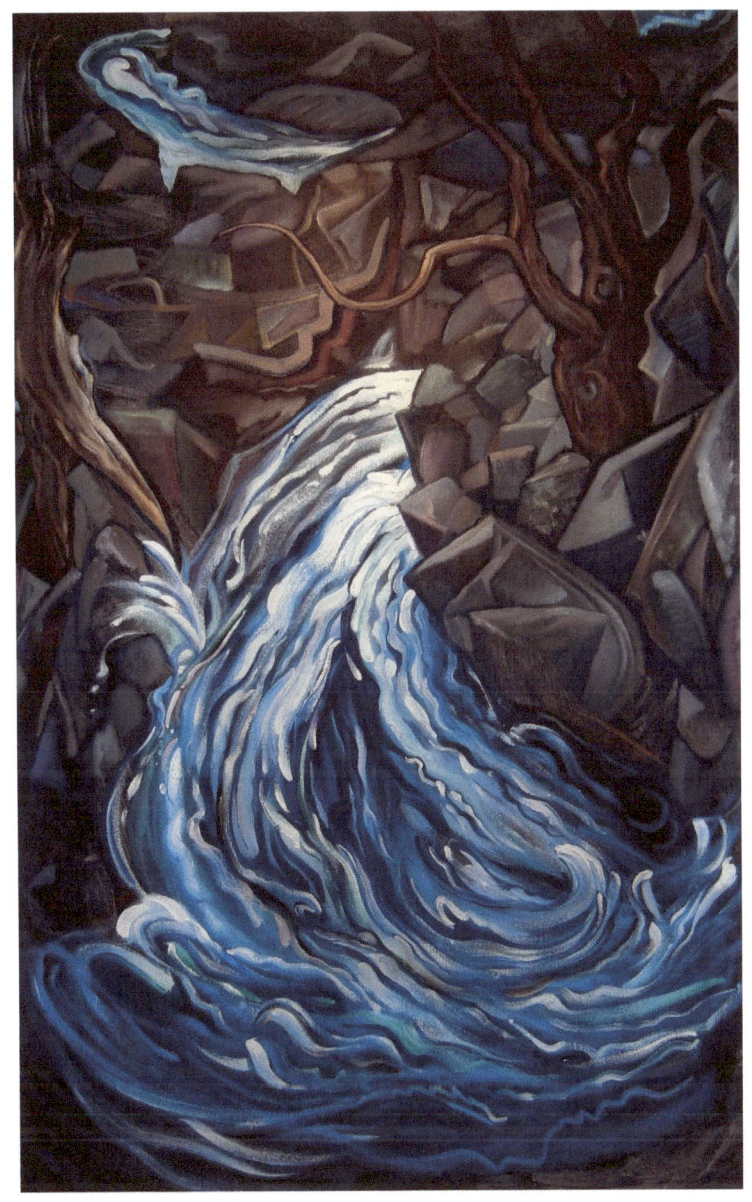

Flood After Fire

Oil on canvas 40x30
2014

For thirty years I have been watching the remains of this old adobe melt in to the earth from where it came. And now it is gone. All that remains are the posts. This is the first of several paintings I have done of it. It gave me a chance to breathe life into what it once was, with color and form suggesting a vivid past.

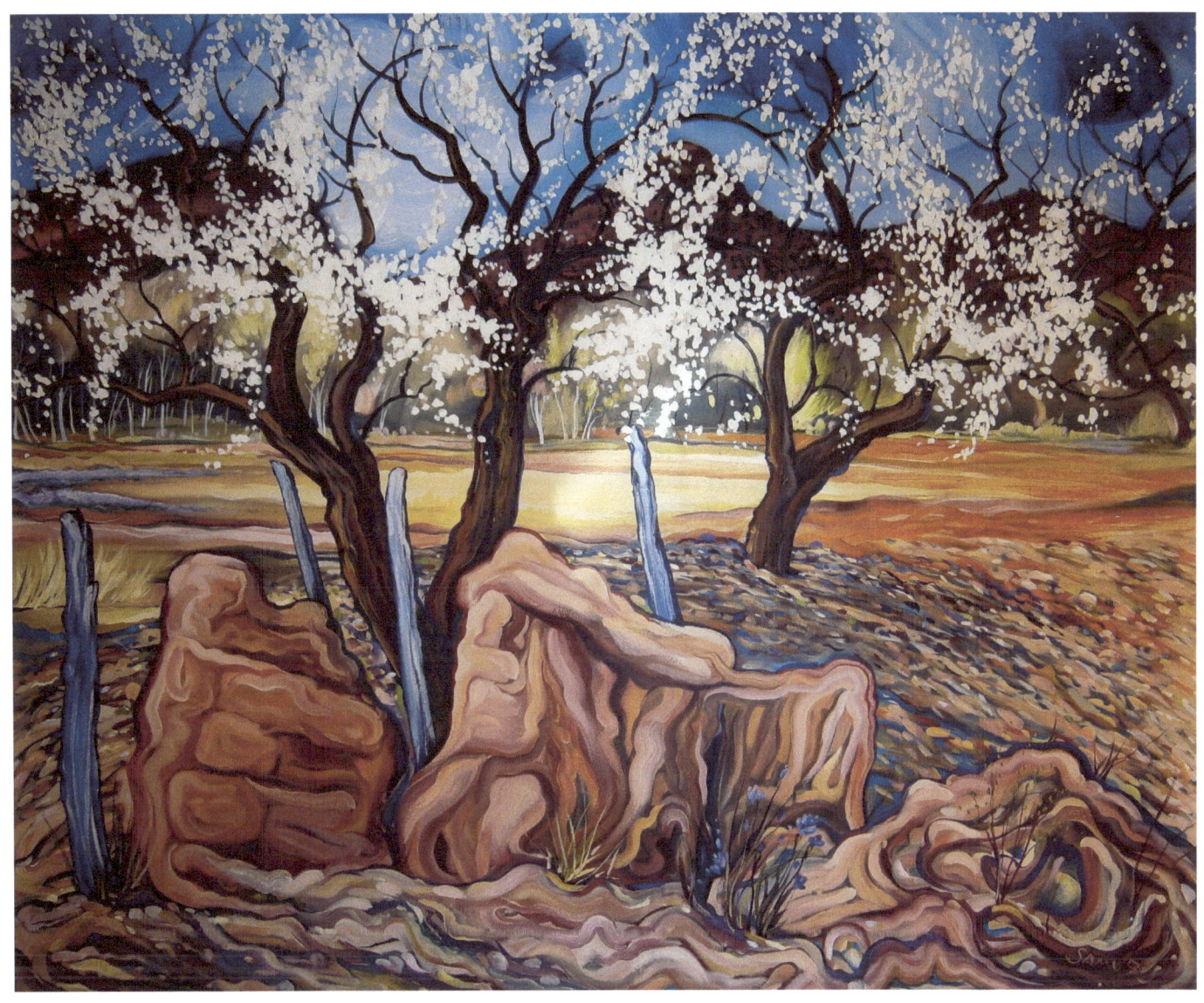

Earth to Earth

Oil on canvas 48x60
2014

I never tire of painting this lovely church. Each time I see it, a surge of energy grips me, to just paint it as fast as I can. I paint it in the afternoon each time, no matter the season. That is when the light hits the west side of the church. It is always a challenge, since the sun's movement changes the shadows with amazing speed, and I have to attack the canvas and spread the paint on it as fast as possible. I love the process, since I get to be lost in the act. It is a wonderful feeling to do so. I guess that is why some call it the creative process. And it is a great place to lose one's self.

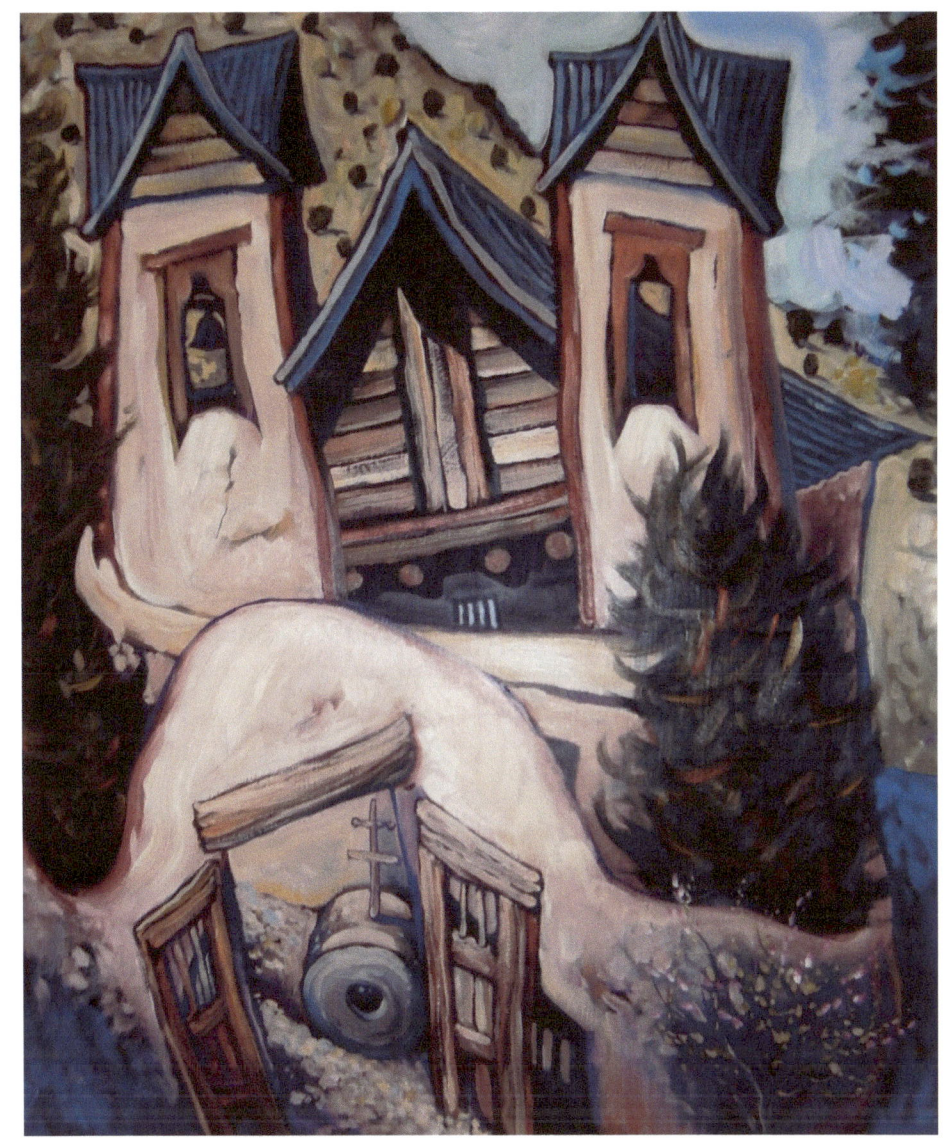

Chimayo Spring

Oil on canvas 30x24
2014

For me, the river is an endless source of wonder and inspiration, always changing and giving the gift of renewal. Exciting in it's beauty, like falling in love each day one sees it.

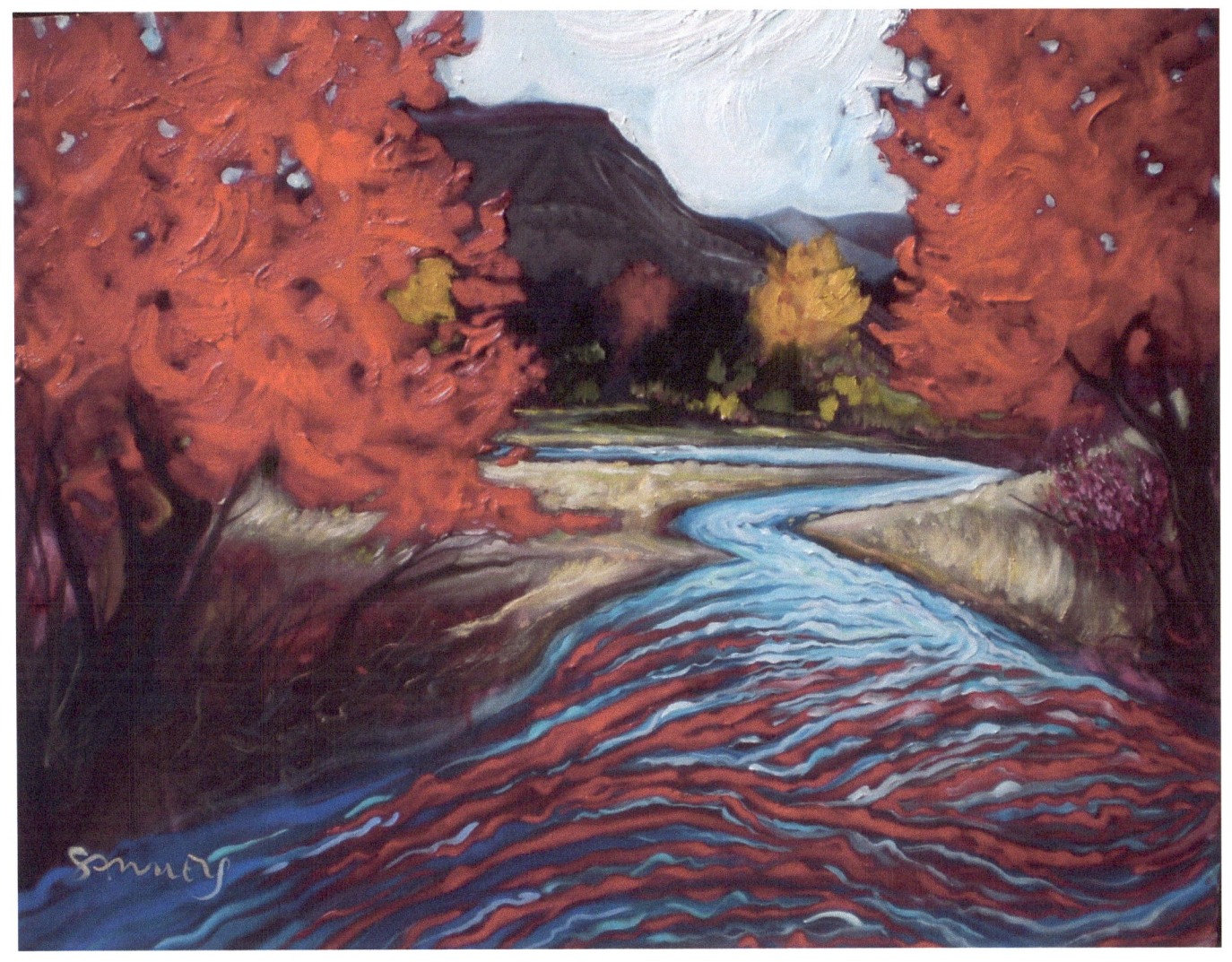

Fall Fire

Oil on canvas 24x30
2014

Yes! The mix of all these textures are just so much fun to interpret. The movement in the sky and the array of colors there. The organic fauna, both living and dead, their growth and demise. And the endless strength of the earth's surface, both emerging and decaying. All with the play of changing light, shafting and speaking as the sun plays on it all. It brings out all the emotions that challenge the artist's need to create. We all love that, and the fruits of that labor: sharing the act and vision.

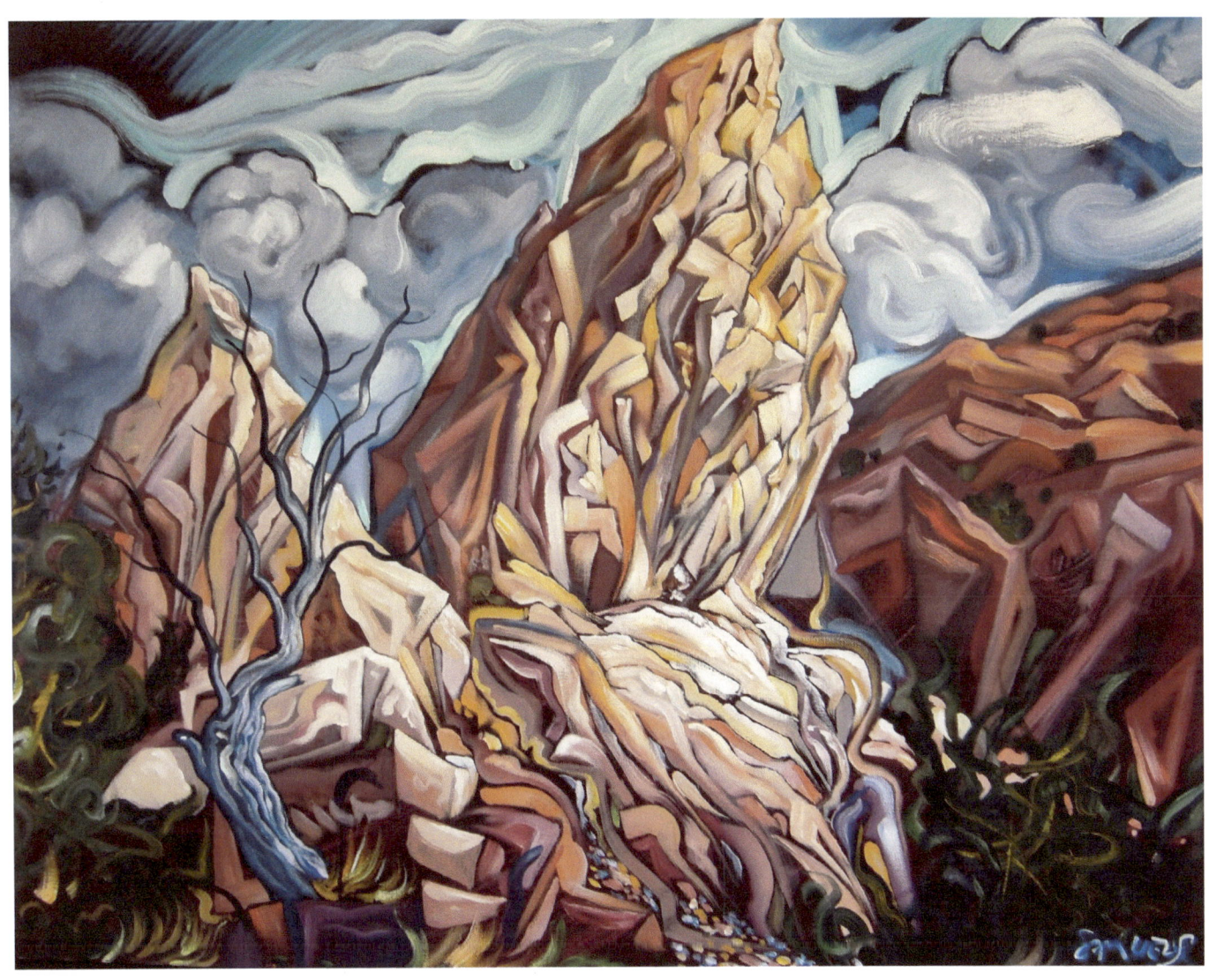

High Road to Madrid

Oil on canvas 30x40
2014

This river is the Snake River, not here in New Mexico, but on the Idaho Border. However, it is a western landscape that I love and have painted several times. I took out the bridge that now stands there, preferring to capture a time gone by. It took quite a while to complete. And it was worth every minute to me when I was done; an endeavor well met and enjoyed.

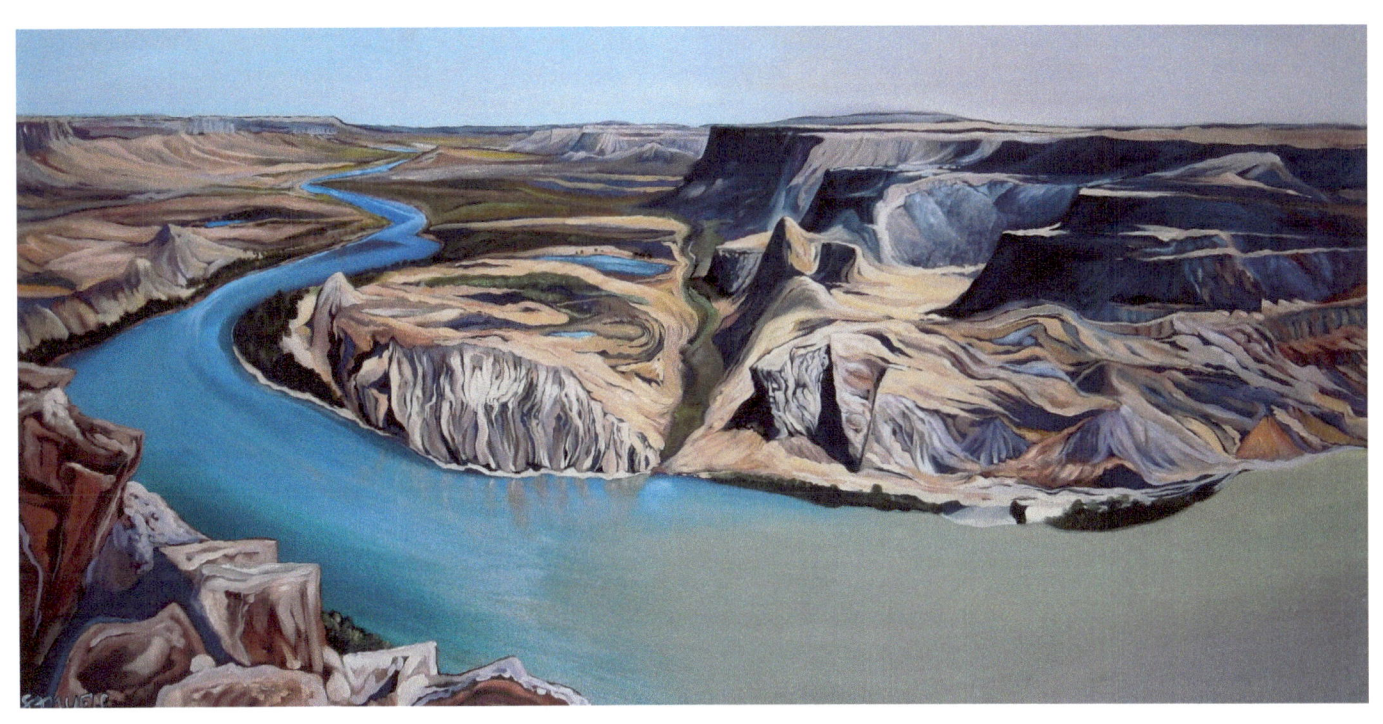

The River

Oil on canvas 24x48
2014

On an off-shoot of my road, there is this old shed with a lovely tree that is in bloom. It is growing as the shed collapses. The mesa in the background is the only part of the earth not eroded by time. All this exists in the now. But all also speaks to what was, long before the spring brought new life. Here in New Mexico, as with much of the southwest, one can see what I have been calling "the Bones of the Earth", given the climate and the lack of water in large part. It gives me the chance to see the contrast and express it in ways not found where I came from. Here one can see thousands if not millions of years existing at the same moment in time, and paint it all together. Now that is fun.

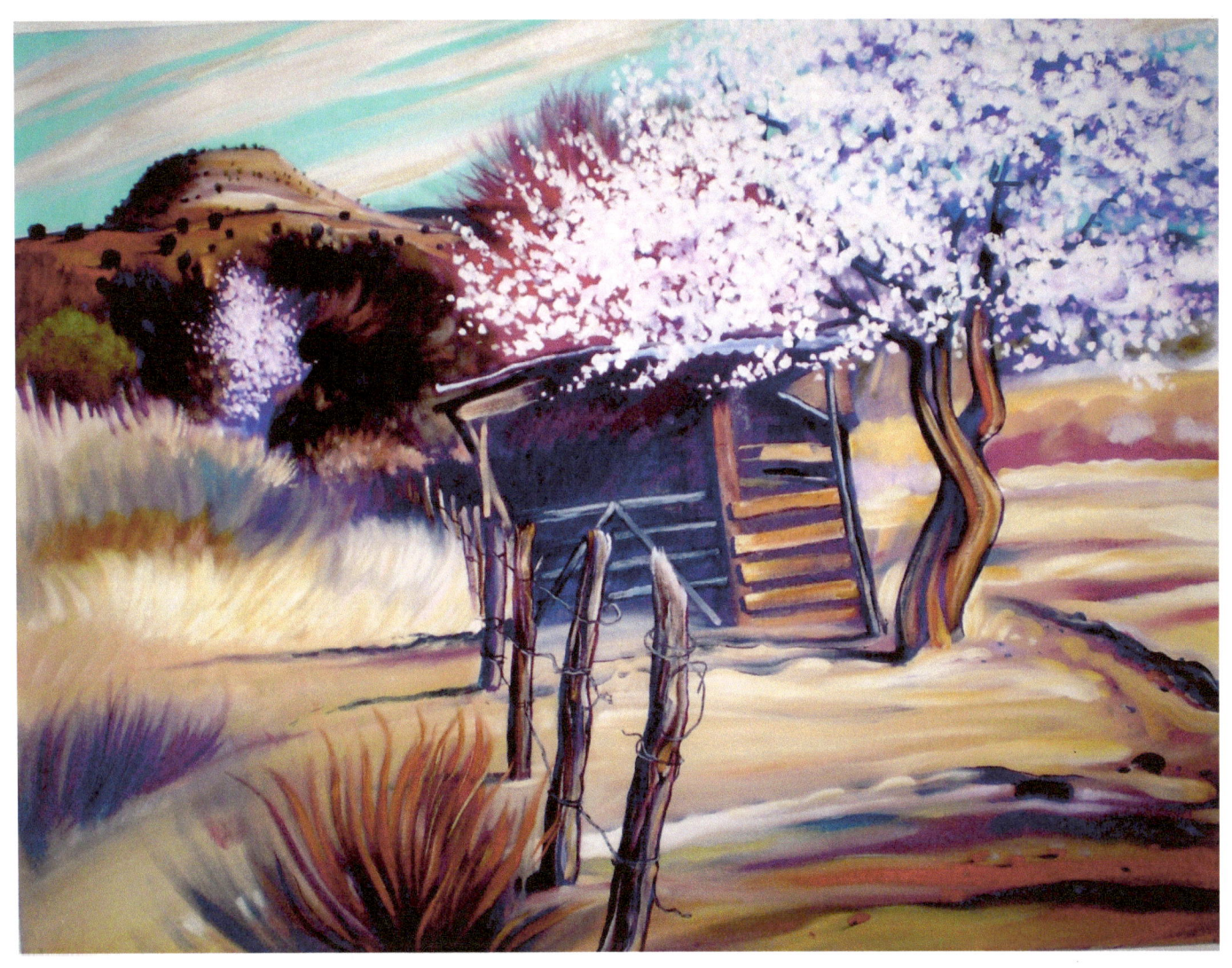

Flood Plain Shed

Oil on canvas 30x40
2014

I paint this view all the time. It never gets to be boring for me. Every year it changes in subtle ways, as do I. In this version I show the calm of a sun lit summer afternoon and the light penetration into the water. Not easy to paint, but little is. I felt that was the theme of this effort, and am pleased to think it worked well.

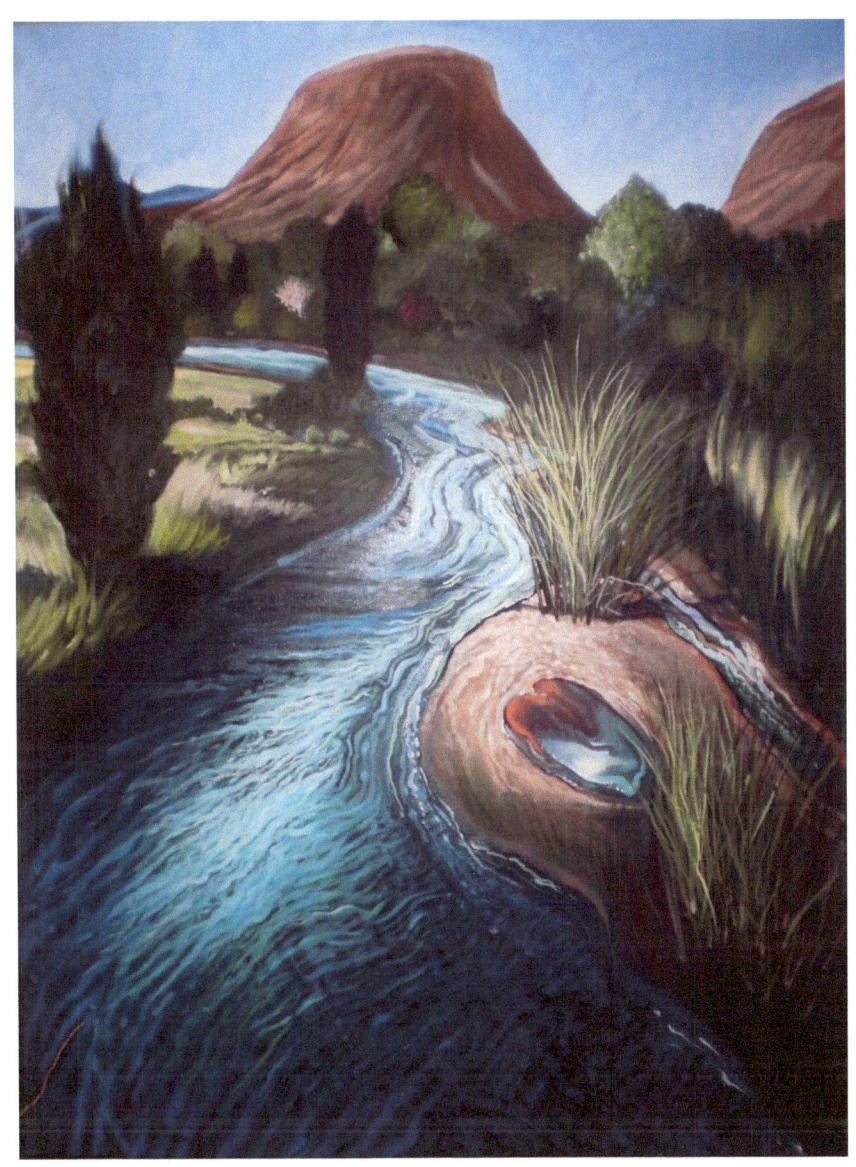

The River Quiet

Oil on canvas 60x44
2014

I love the juxtaposition of water activity in the desert wilds of New Mexico. Here it is in the falls at Nambe Pueblo. A wonderful double waterfalls to paint on site. Hearing the surge of water over the cliffs is just great to paint to; music that lifts the artist spirit.

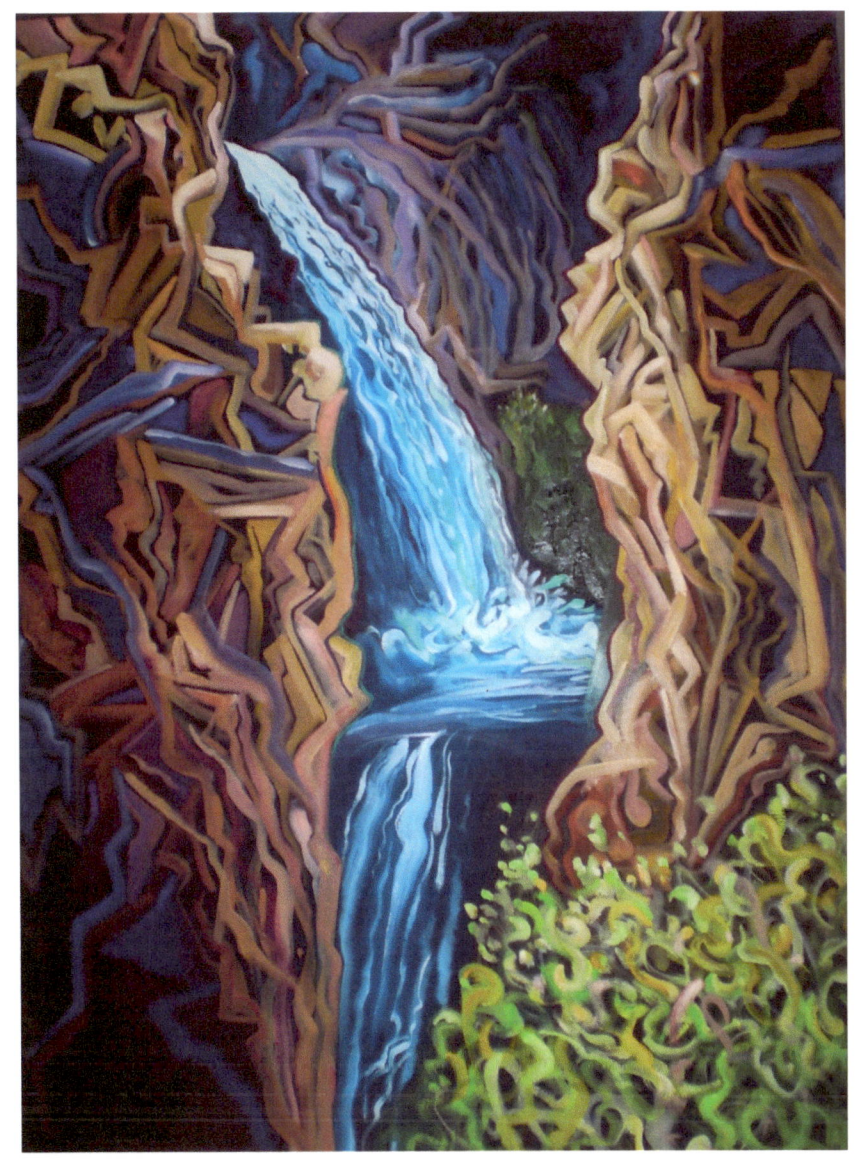

Nambe Falls

Oil on canvas 40x30
2014

I come from one of the largest cities in the world. And yet, seem to find almost all my subjects to paint within a 10 mile radius, here in the Jemez Mountains. I just love it. This creek is often dry, but of late we have had quite a lot of moisture. So I get to paint it often, in all it's reflective beauty.

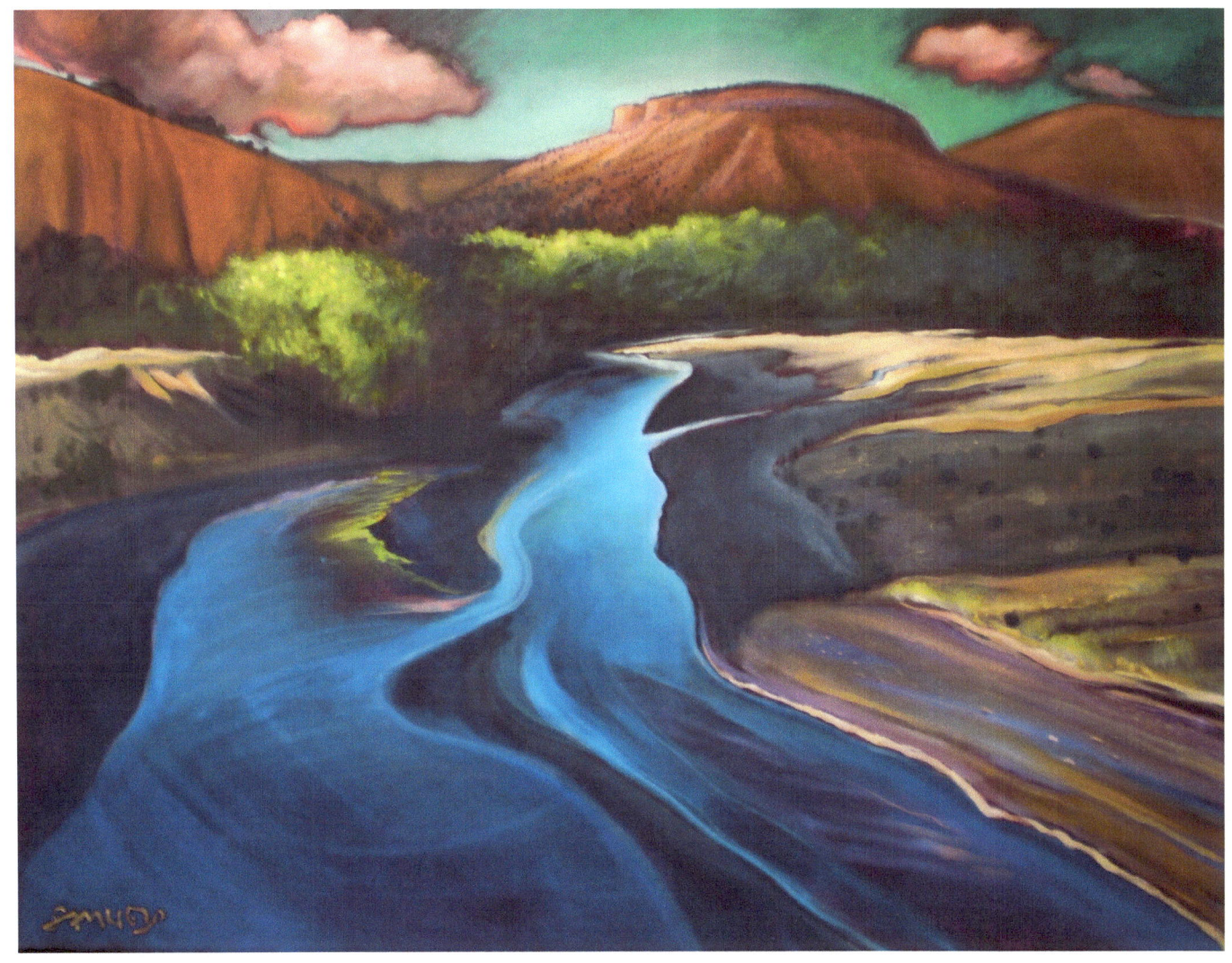

Ponderosa Creek

Oil on canvas 40x30
2014

Again, the view from the Bridge across which I travel every day. An endless source of subject matter for my artist eyes. Is it no wonder that after traveling the world over, that I am here in The Island In The Sky, so nicely put by the PBS special on these Jemez Mountains. And this, the season of Jemez Gold. Already, I have several more compositions in mind for the next paintings. How blessed to be living here in this place of beauty.

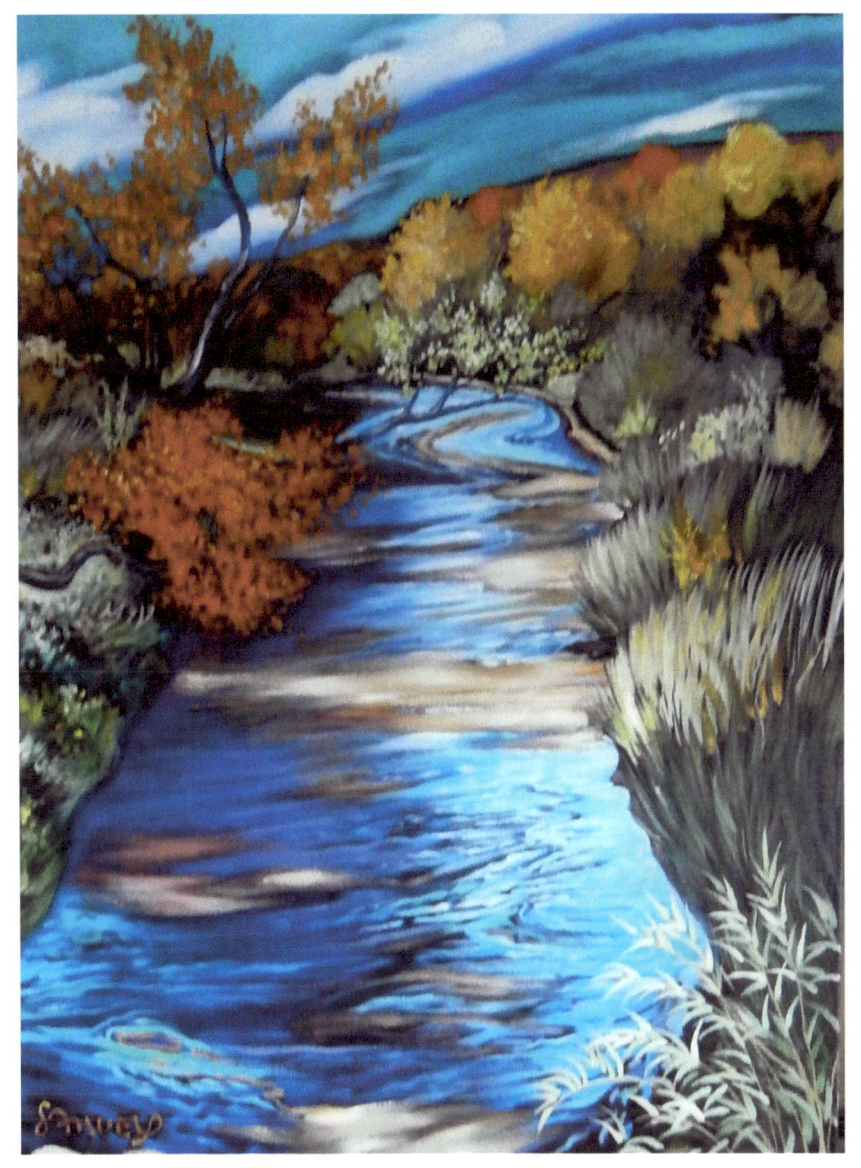

Orange Day   Oil on canvas 40x30
2014

I have painted these two Adobes, about a mile from my home, several times. And each time, the painting is so different from the one before. I got myself very excited as it was coming to a close. I just love how it turned out this time.

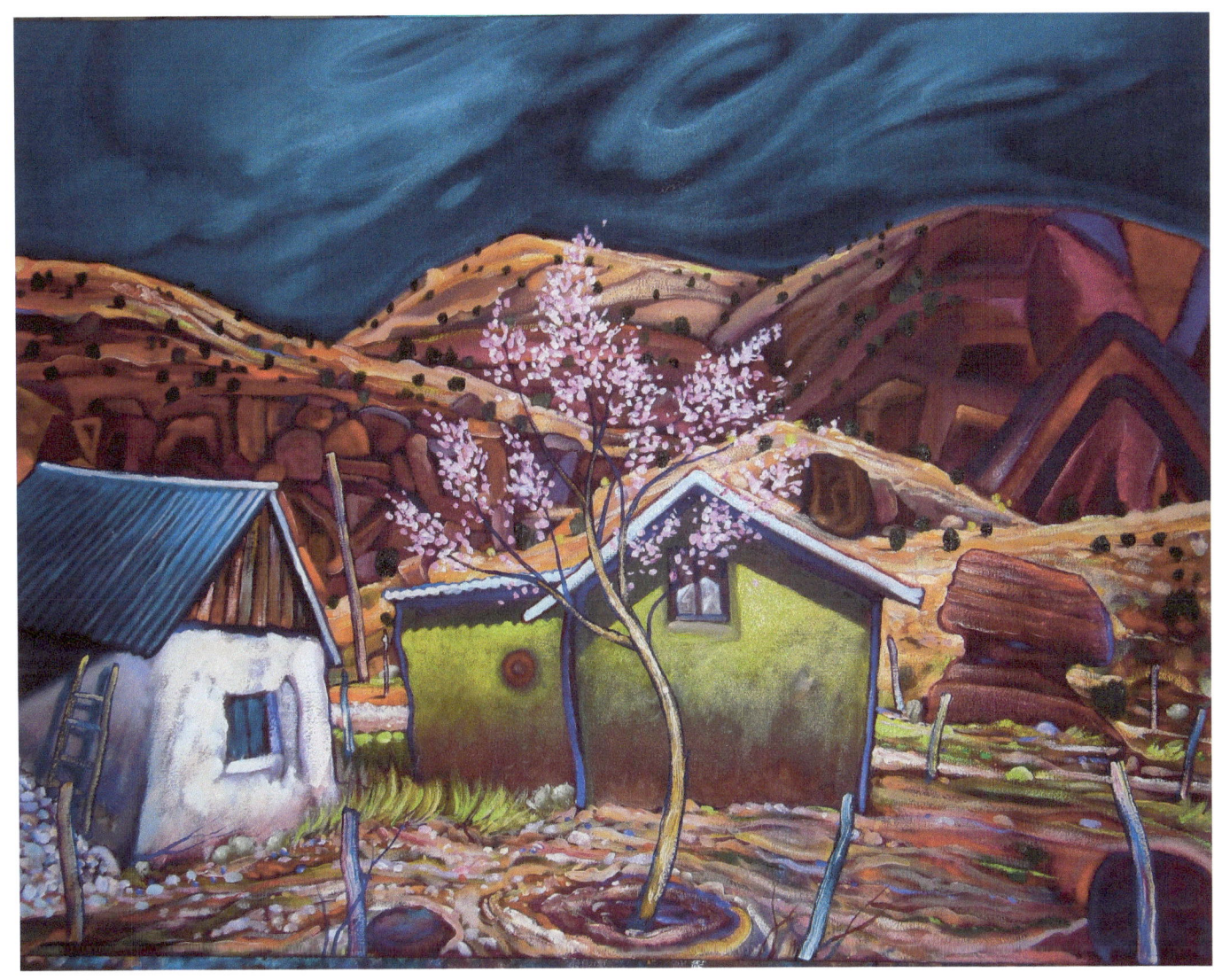

Green Adobe

Oil on canvas 30x40
2014

When I visit my daughter Dagna's family in Jemez Springs, I often see their grand views as new subject matter for me. Here is the view of their arroyo, facing north. The atmosphere lit by the southern sun was great that day. I took home my photos and did this one. Any painting is a challenge. But each day I awake thinking, what will it be today?

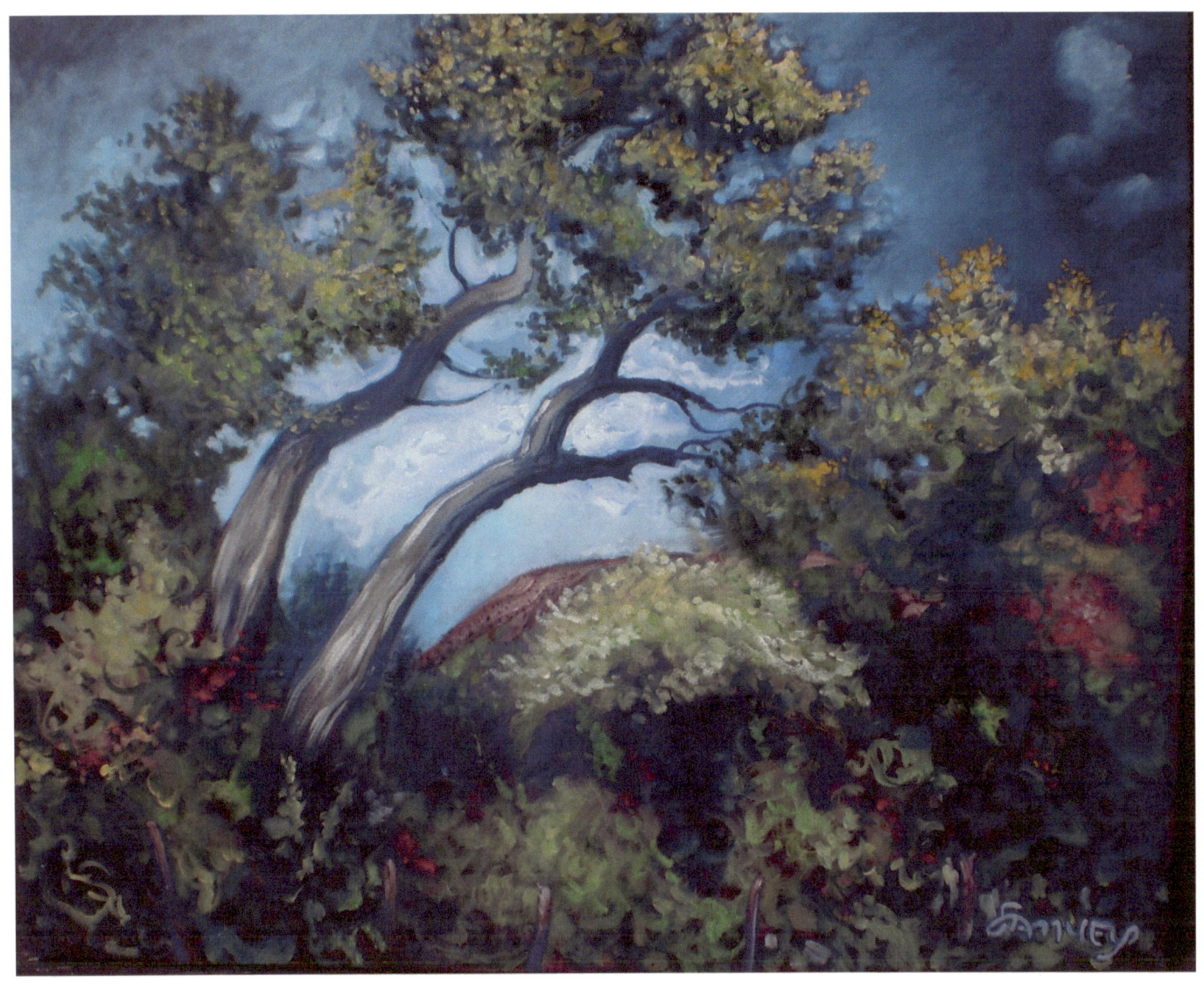

Arroyo View

Oil on canvas 24x30
2014

The house on the left is now gone. It was where Don Lucero, the patriarch of the Lucero's was born. He made his mark in these valleys, including building a church that I often paint. After he passed, his new son-in-law tore it down. A shame, but it was the model for many paintings before it was gone. He was a dear friend and helped me settle into this beautiful valley.

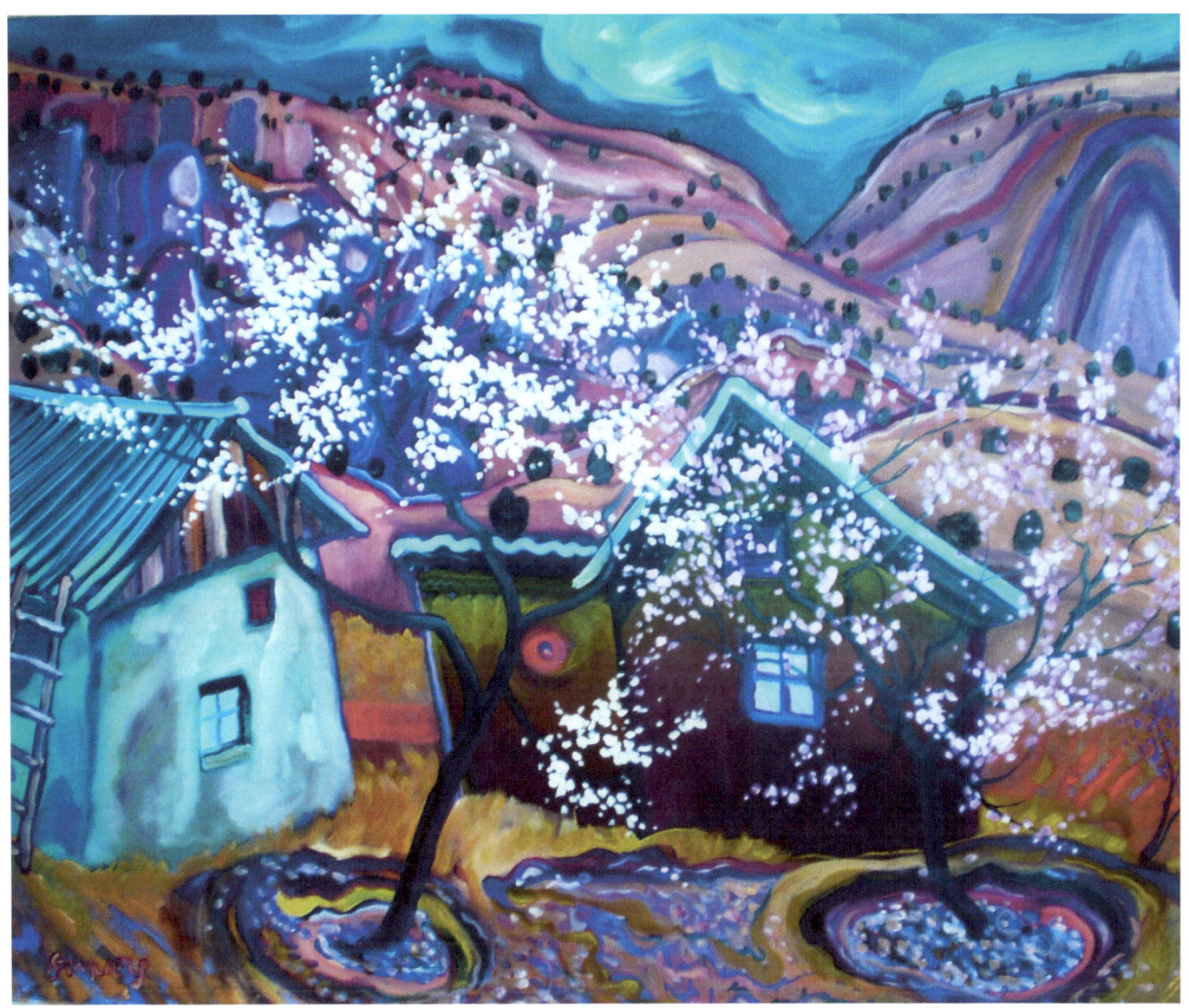

Newly Planted

Oil on canvas 24x30
2014

This is the view from my porch after an Autumn rain storm. The view is down the road south, from the third story porch of my home. Nice to be able to set up out there and get some painting done without leaving the house. Every window or door has a great view. I told a neighbor once we all have the best view. And for the most part, it is true. I love living here.

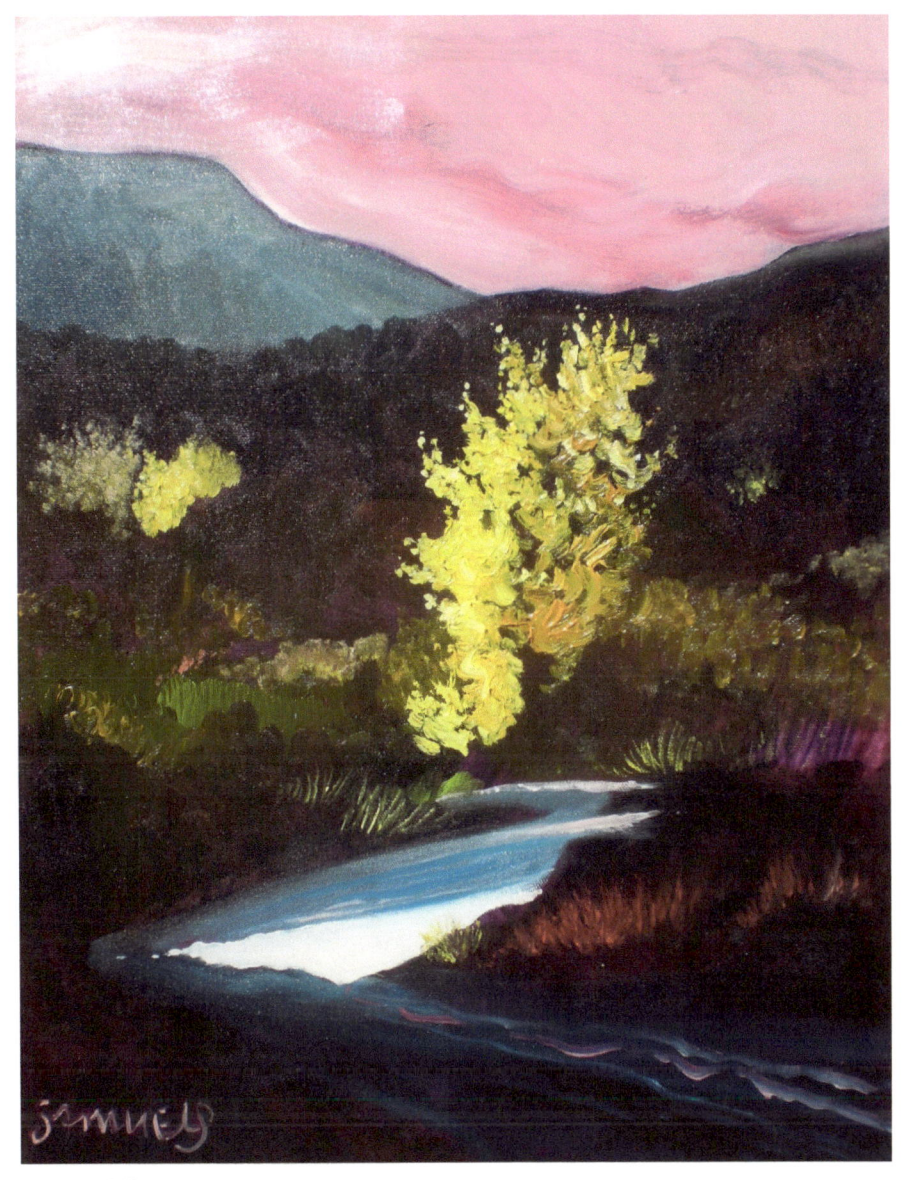

Porch View

Oil on canvas 30x24
2014

This was a small on-site sketch that started the series of bell tower paintings. It is down the road three miles. And when coming home in the early morning, I was stunned by the sunrise hitting the church and bell tower. I never had seen it in the morning light before. It ushered in a group of works that I am still painting.

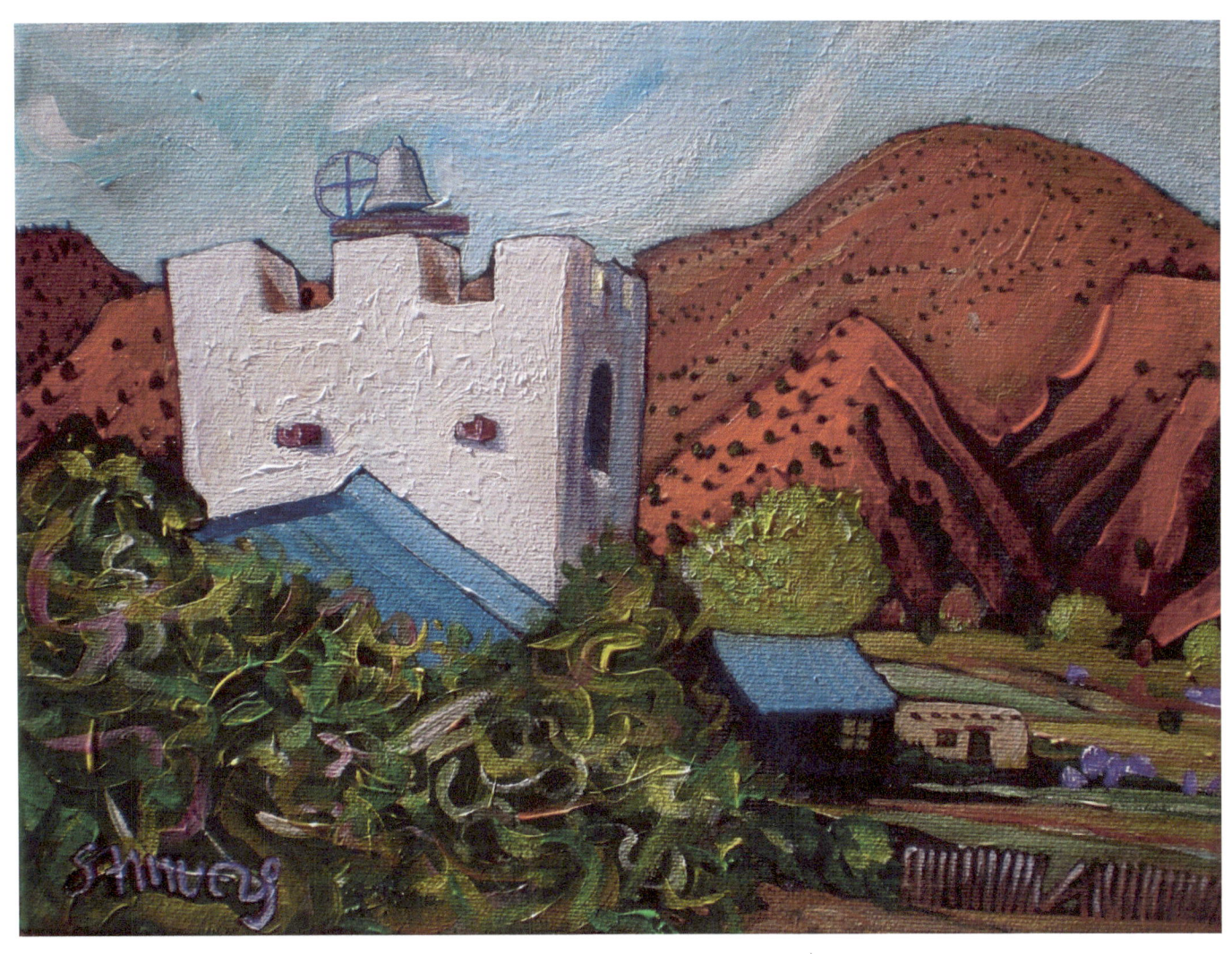

Small Bell Tower

Oil on canvas 9x12
2014

The light playing on this old barn, which is still standing, down the road a mile, at sunset is yet another perfect subject for my work. That it still stands is quite enough reason. But as usual everything here, by where I choose to live, it speaks to me in such a way that I never want to stop listening.

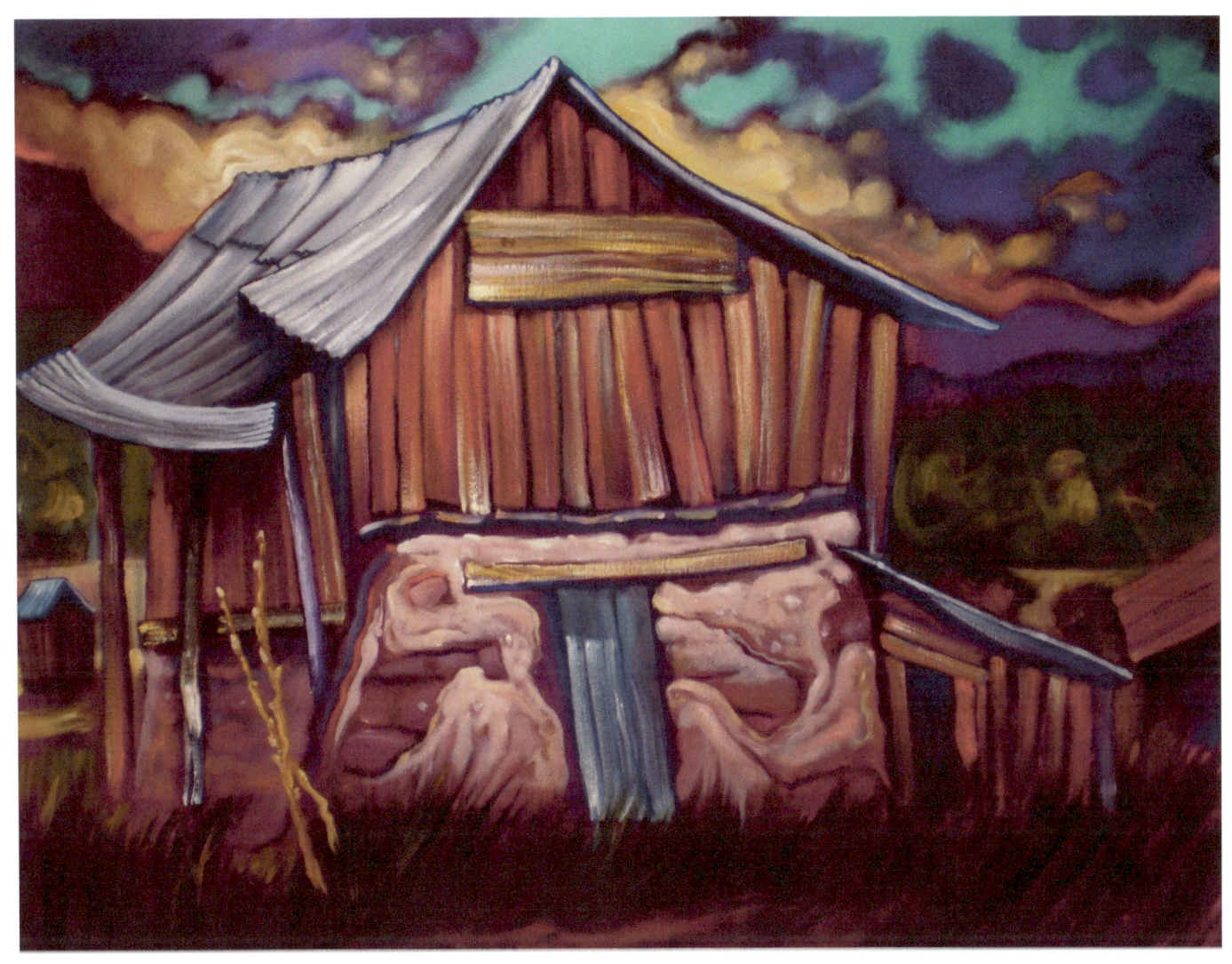

Summer

Oil on canvas 24x30
2014

This Jemez Mountain spring fed pool is called McCauly Spring. The Jemez mountains' last addition was the volcano's eruption a million years ago. Scott Momaday calls the Jemez, "The Island In The Sky". And, PBS made it a documentary film. I love the clarity of the springs water and the big black obsidian boulders encircling it. I spent a year on this one, glazing and painting layer upon layer to get the liquidity of the water and the endless reflections playing on the surface. I stop for now, but probably could paint another year on it and still enjoy myself, but then it would be a different painting.

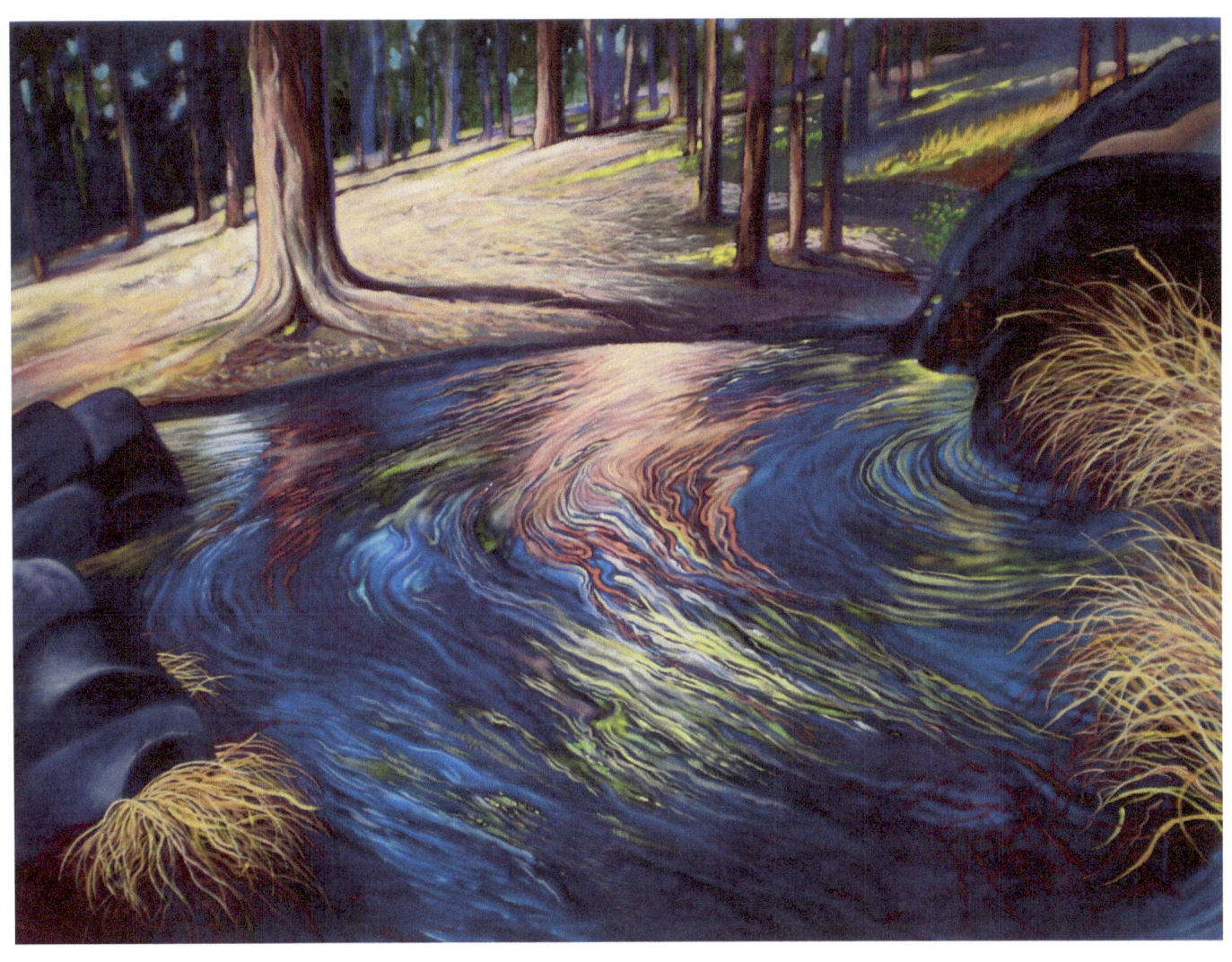

Obsidian Pool

Oil on canvas 44x60
2014

The Santerio de Chimayo is a wonderful place where I have had so many enlightening experiences, as well as inspirational ones. But the fact remains that when I am there, I paint like it's the last one. The sun sets so fast in that little valley. Right behind me on the western hill. It is a race to get the image down since the shadows move so fast, but always worth it. It is such a wonderful feeling when the race is over. Then I pack up the easel and head home. Arriving home, I get the painting hung up and finish it off. Like bringing the experience home with me.

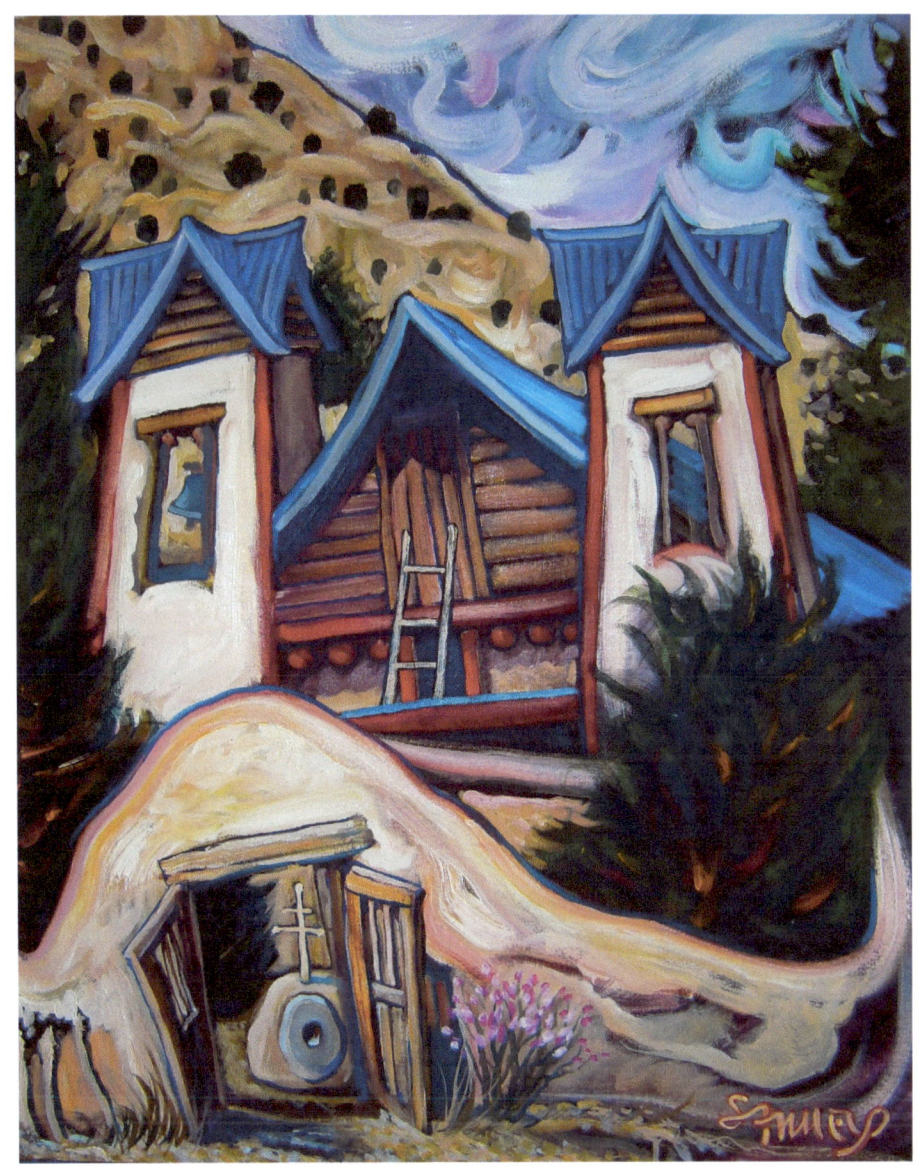

Chimayo

Oil on canvas 30X24
2014

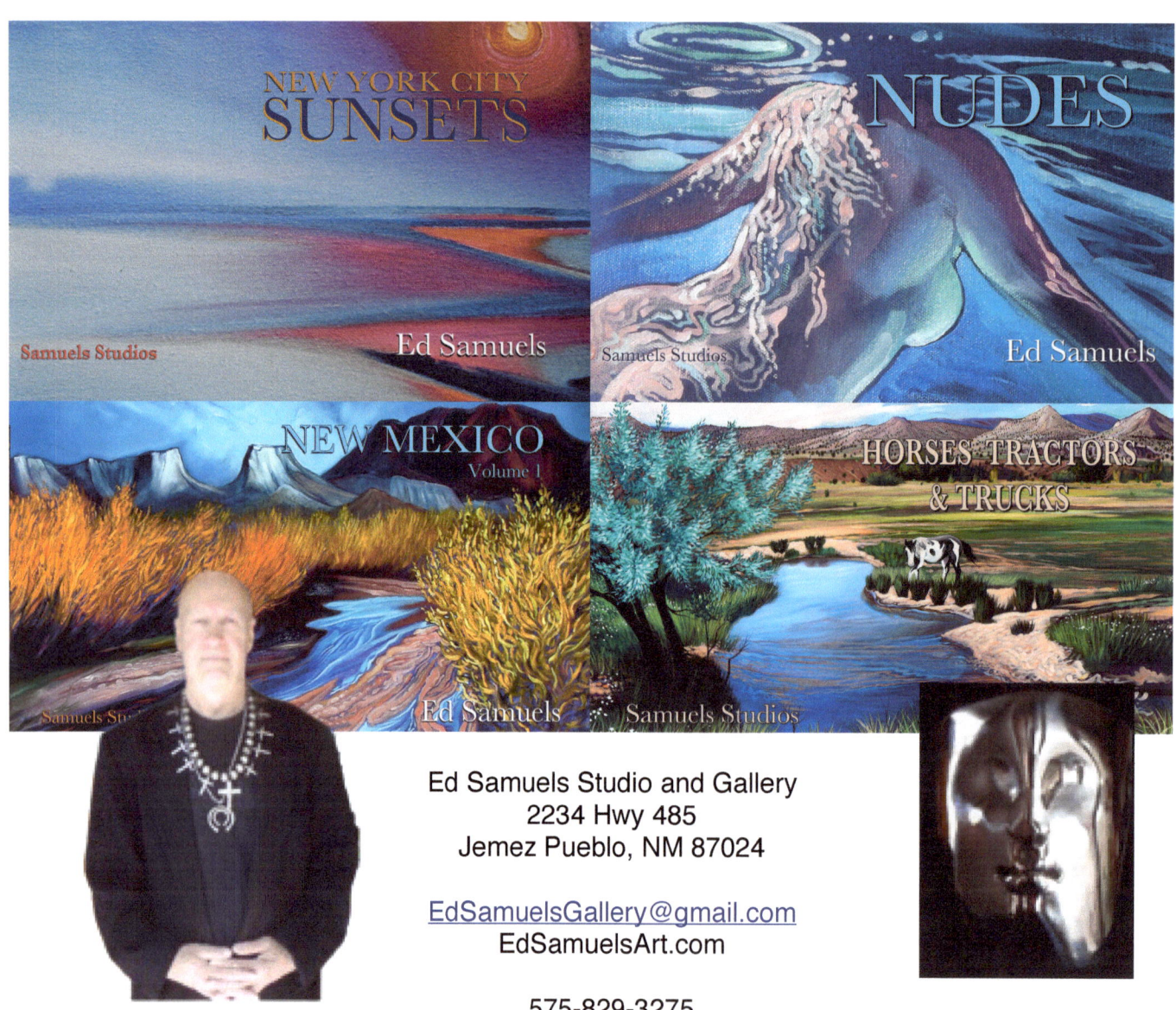

Ed Samuels Studio and Gallery
2234 Hwy 485
Jemez Pueblo, NM 87024

EdSamuelsGallery@gmail.com
EdSamuelsArt.com

575-829-3275

www.ingramcontent.com/pod-product-compliance
Lightning Source LLC
Chambersburg PA
CBHW040742200526
45159CB00023B/1468